Every Man's Conscience

"*Every Man's Conscience* is a needed addition to the growing library of Christian Endurance studies. King's work provides a window into Baptist history that helps the contemporary Christian recognize the dangers of accommodating state churches and antagonistic cultures. It acknowledges the role government has played in both liberty and persecution, while parsing the distractions and theological errors the church has continually faced. *Every Man's Conscience* is not just for Baptists, but for any Christian from a Kingdom-oriented tradition who wants to increase trust in Christ's infinite capacity to fulfill his promises under any—and all—cultural circumstances."

K.A. ELLIS
Director of The Edmiston Center,
Reformed Theological Seminary, Atlanta

"Since the early seventeenth century, the struggle for religious liberty has been a regular, if not always consistent, feature of Baptist testimony. As Ryan King's new book demonstrates, in wonderful historical detail, this commitment to liberty has shaped in profound ways Baptist thinking about church and state—and offers a powerful alternative to the Scylla and Charybdis of unprincipled relativism and inflexible hegemony."

CRAWFORD GRIBBEN
Professor of History,
Queen's University Belfast

"As a Reformed Baptist, and a devoted student of the English Civil War, I have sometimes reflected that Parliament's Blasphemy Ordinance of 1648 would have sent me either to prison or the gallows. Our Presbyterian forefathers (who dominated Parliament at that time) were not renowned for religious toleration. It fell to Baptists and their allies to make the robust case for toleration. In this significant work, Ryan King documents the noble and principled Baptist commitment to religious liberty in the story of Christian and Protestant history. I commend the work very warmly."

NICK NEEDHAM
Church History Tutor, Highland Theological College;
Author of the series *2000 Years of Christ's Power*

"Ryan King has produced an impressive piece of work, detailed in its research and addressing the vitally important subject of religious freedom and as such it is timely. We are facing new challenges to our testimony to the truth from postmodernism and particularly the LGBTQ lobby. It is good to be turned to those who have gone before and to be inspired by their faithful witness. Our theological forebears paid a high price for religious freedom. I am happy to commend this work."

ROBERT W. OLIVER
Author of *History of the English Calvinistic Baptists 1771-1892*

"Religious freedom is a vital topic—historically and currently. This excellent book guides the reader along the contours of the world in which early Baptists found themselves, and through which they forged a uniquely biblical and nuanced path. Meticulously researched, vividly written, and sensitively applied to the contemporary world, this is a wise guide to what our Baptist forbears wrestled with in their age, and what we must grapple with in our own."

ANDREW ROYCROFT
Pastor, Portadown Baptist Church, County Armagh, Ireland;
Visiting lecturer in Biblical Theology & Apologetics, Irish Baptist College

"Given recent shifts in Western culture, it is understandable that Christians feel the pressing need to understand the church's relationship to the government. What is needed in our day is not manmade knee-jerk reactions and short-sighted solutions, but rather sober trust in the sovereign God's covenantal and eschatological promises. In this book, Ryan King offers such sobriety by showing how major Baptists in history have thought about religious liberty and how Baptist history can help Christians (even non-Baptists!) engage the government and culture wisely today. Highly recommended!"

BRANDON D. SMITH
Associate Professor Theology Early Christianity and Chair of the Herschel H. Hobbs School of Theology and Ministry, Oklahoma Baptist University;
Cofounder, the Center for Baptist Renewal

STUDIES IN BAPTIST HISTORY

EVERY MAN'S CONSCIENCE

*Early English Baptists
and the Fight for Religious Liberty*

RYAN BURTON KING

Every Man's Conscience: Early English Baptists and the Fight for Religious Liberty

Copyright © 2024 Ryan Burton King. All rights reserved.
This book may not be reproduced, in whole or in part, without written permission from the publishers.

Studies in Baptist History, Volume 4

H&E Academic, West Lorne, Ontario
www.hesedandemet.com

Paperback ISBN: 978-1-77484-149-5
eBook ISBN: 978-1-77484-147-1

For my parents,
Barry and Frances King

Then Jesus said to him,
"Put your sword back into its place.
For all who take the sword will perish by the sword."
Matthew 26:52

Jesus answered,
"My kingdom is not of this world. If my kingdom were of this world, my servants would have been fighting, that I might not be delivered over to the Jews. But my kingdom is not from the world."
John 18:36

CONTENTS

Foreword iii
   Malcolm B. Yarnell III

Introduction: Religious Liberty—a Baptist Distinctive 1

Part One
The Crucible of Persecution: Surveying the Historical Context

1. Persecution of Continental Baptistic Movements 9
2. Persecution of the Early English Baptists 13
3. Persecution of Non-Christians 17

Part Two
Preaching, not persecuting: Early General Baptists

4. John Smyth 25
5. Thomas Helwys 31
6. Leonard Busher 37
7. John Murton 45

Part Three
Endeavouring to Have a Clear Conscience: Early Particular Baptists

8. Particular Baptist Origins 49
9. Roger Williams 53
10. The First London Baptist Confession 59
11. Samuel Richardson 61
12. Particular Baptist Religious Liberty—for Everyone? 65
13. Christopher Blackwood 73
14. Thomas Collier 79
15. The Second London Baptist Confession 85
16. Liberty? 91

Conclusion 97
Acknowledgements 103
Bibliography 105
Subject Index 117

Foreword
For Your Freedom of Conscience

Malcolm B. Yarnell III

Every Man's Conscience will be one of the most valuable texts you ever read. The author addresses an extremely important subject to you: You and your most fundamental right, your personal freedom of conscience. Sadly, liberty of conscience has become a subject too often neglected by many who should know better even while it is being attacked by those who would bring harm to humanity.

This book addresses your personal freedom before other people and your personal right (and responsibility) to seek out and retain eternal truth as you deem best. Through thoughtful historical commentary, Ryan Burton King wants us to understand how liberty of conscience is the inalienable possession and responsibility of every human being. King has collected rare texts from an early modern intellectual tradition which helped to shape modernity's conceptions about human dignity, human freedom, and human rights. And he explains why those concepts remain important for the world in which we live today.

A few words about why this book is necessary, a short description of the lineaments of the genius which it affirms, and an expression of appreciation may help launch your reading.

Why This Book Is Necessary Now

It has been widely affirmed that if the fundamental modern idea of liberty of conscience is diminished, then our other rights will come under pressure, and our ability to pursue human flourishing will be inhibited. Standing on opposing sides of a worldwide religious tradition, both the Roman Catholic Pope John Paul II and free church Baptists together recognize that liberty in the matter of religion is the first freedom upon which all other human freedoms depend.[1]

---

[1] John Paul II to the heads of state of the nations who signed the Helsinki Final Act (1975), September 1, 1980, on the eve of the Madrid Conference on European Security and Cooperation,

Foreword

Human beings across the world, whether they hold to Christian, Hindu, Muslim, Jewish, or Atheistic worldviews, increasingly agree that human rights must be respected. The United Nations Declaration on Human Rights was written and has been widely accepted due to the burgeoning hope that all nations will embrace the fundamental importance of human dignity and will recognize basic human rights. Despite their widespread affirmation across cultures, various scholars have demonstrated how those rights nevertheless began to be recognized in a specific historical context.[2] This book addresses a critical movement in that context.

This book could not have appeared at a more propitious moment, for these very ideas are under attack from multiple directions. On the one hand, adherents to various religions in the contemporary West face an assault on their liberty of conscience from elements of the radical political Left. Some hope to limit religious believers' human rights by restricting religious expression to private worship or private opinion. They argue for the priority of their own sexual expression over religious liberty and religious action.[3]

On the other hand, the assault on religious liberty comes not merely from the Left. A potentially devastating and deceptive assault also comes from elements of the radical Right. Proponents of a new strain of "Christian Nationalism" may prove particularly deceptive in the churches because they audaciously use the name of God and propose to enthrone Christ over culture. These proponents draw upon harmful ideas once advocated by medieval thinkers, intolerant Puritans, slaveholding theologians, and modern reconstructionists.[4]

Ryan King is sensitive in this book, not only to discuss the lessons learned by others in the past but to the needs of our present day, needs that require the

---

no. 5; Jason G. Duesing, Thomas White, and Malcolm B. Yarnell III, eds., *First Freedom: The Beginning and End of Religious Liberty*, 2nd ed. (Nashville, TN: B&H Academic, 2016).

[2] Tom Holland, *Dominion: How the Christian Revolution Remade the World* (New York: Basic Books, 2019); Larry Siedentop, *Inventing the Individual: The Origins of Western Liberalism* (New York: Allen Lane, 2014); John Witte, Jr. and Frank S. Alexander eds., *Christianity and Human Rights: An Introduction* (Cambridge: Cambridge University Press, 2010).

[3] Mary Eberstadt, *It's Dangerous to Believe: Religious Freedom and Its Enemies* (San Francisco: Harper, 2016); Luke Goodrich, *Free to Believe: The Battle Over Religious Liberty in America* (Colorado Springs: Multnomah, 2019).

[4] Stephen Wolfe, *The Case for Christian Nationalism* (Moscow, ID: Canon Press, 2022). See the critiques by Kevin DeYoung, "The Rise of Right-Wing Wokeism," *The Gospel Coalition* (November 2022); Paul Matzko, "Beware the 'Christian Prince,'" *Reason: Free Minds and Free Markets* (June 2023); Andrew T. Walker, "Book Review: The Case for Christian Nationalism," *Nine Marks* (November 2022).

appearance of this book now. Indeed, it could be argued that part of the problem in the present is that many of the religious heirs of the intellectual tradition which King discloses are themselves unaware of their own founding genius. If we were more aware of our past, we might be even more willing to oppose expressions of intolerance or racism and ethnocentrism than we already are.

The Lineaments of Liberty of Conscience

If the reader will allow it, I want to reaffirm and restate in my own words the religious genius of the tradition King exposits so well in this book. Even if the reader is secular in outlook, it must be recognized that the radicals who helped foster the rise of the modern discourse on universal human rights acted from ideas arising from their religious faith. For many of these radical believers, the truths they discovered were so significant that they were willing not only to endure social disapproval but to suffer government persecution, even to the point of death. These Christians believed above all in Jesus Christ as their Lord, King, and Master. Several other doctrines accompanied or flowed from their primary belief in the sole Lordship of Jesus Christ.

First, these Non-conformists pursued with all their heart, soul, mind, and strength the basic and exclusive Christian confession that *Jesus Christ is the one Lord* (John 14:6; Rom. 10:9-10; 1 Cor. 12:3). Dissenting men and women advocated liberty of conscience precisely because they believed the second person of the divine Trinity had become human, died on a cross, and then arose from death. They had encountered Christ personally, been called to forsake their rebellion against God, and responded by taking up their crosses and following their master as his disciples (Mark 8:34-38). The free church doctrine of liberty of conscience is grounded in a series of faith claims, but the first and foremost dogma for them was that Jesus Christ, as the true Lord, is the only one who can demand loyalty from a human soul.

Second, they believed the Lordship of Jesus and all other necessary doctrines are clearly taught in the Christian canon, the Holy Bible. *Scripture alone*, working by the Holy Spirit, is sufficient to accomplish the spiritual purposes for which the church of Jesus Christ exists. Because they believed his Word was sufficient to meet Christ's purpose for the church in spreading the faith, they identified any attempt to spread Christianity by means of coercion through government as showing lack of faith in Jesus Christ. Christ commanded his church to use the great authority of the sword of the Spirit, which is the Word of God (Eph. 6:10-18). The Word of God itself, illumined by the

Foreword

Holy Spirit, has sufficient power to convert human souls (1 Peter 1:22-25; 2 Peter 1:16-21). The great authority of the sword of the flesh, which restrains wickedness through violence, rightfully belongs not to the church but to the state alone (Rom. 13:1-7).

Third, they believed in the necessity of salvation by grace alone through *personal faith alone* in Christ alone. In reading and hearing Scripture carefully, they discovered that Jesus was establishing his kingdom upon the earth now and will bring his kingdom in its fullness one day. In agreement with the Reformers, they believed that they needed to unite with Christ personally through being born again into a saving relation by faith alone (Rom. 1:16-17). They read that every human being is personally responsible for their acts and will be held accountable before God (Ezek. 18; Rev. 20:11-15), a foreboding truth to which every human conscience testifies even now (Rom. 2:15-16). This personal faith in Jesus Christ as Lord means that no other person ought to impinge upon faith. Christ alone is the mediator between God and man, so he alone must be given personal faith and faithful loyalty (1 Tim. 2:5-6).

Fourth, arising from their loyal faith in Christ as Lord, they believed that *Christ alone rules the church*. Christ is present to each locally covenanted church, which must be governed by his discipline alone (Matt. 18:15-20). His ordinances, including baptism and the Lord's Supper, must be obeyed as revealed in Scripture without subtraction, addition, or other alteration. Before communion may be taken, baptism must be given to believers only, for each conscience must testify its personal faith to God (Matt. 28:18-20; 1 Peter 3:21). With Paul, they believed the demonic "mystery of iniquity" is already at work and should be ascribed to any attempt to put another person or institution in the place of God (2 Thess. 2:4, 7). This included, of course, any attempt to impose laws advocated by a pope, a king, a presbytery, or a pastor upon a church and upon a conscience. Their faith required a reevaluation of every human tradition, including those which had been built up around the sacraments and the governance of the church by those they deemed usurpers.

Fifth, these radical Christians' loyalty to Christ as the only lord of the human conscience and as the only head of the church led them to advocate the *separation of church and state*. They appealed to the words of Jesus that a distinction must be made between what is owed to Caesar and what is owed to God (Matt. 22:15-22). They also argued that the responsibility to judge human bodies for holding certain beliefs belongs not to human beings but to God alone. They departed from the persecutory reading of Matthew 13:24-30 which had been advanced by Augustine, the medieval church, John Calvin, and the Puritans, among others. Instead, they showed how Jesus taught that the judgment of unbelievers in the world was to occur at the end of the world and was to be executed by his angels. These radical Christians rejected the longstanding Christian tradition of religious persecution by appealing to the true interpretation of the parable, which was taught by the Lord himself (Matt. 13:36–43).

Thanksgiving
For those radical Christians whom we know today as the Continental Anabaptists, the early English Baptists, the early American Baptists, the Quakers, and others, we should be thankful. We should be thankful that they corrected the major Christian traditions, who had brought untold misery upon human beings through persecuting bodies to maintain or advance their own ideas. Now, rather than oppressing consciences through forcing bodies, Christians widely recognize the churches' responsibility is not to *persecute* but to *persuade*. We must honor the sanctity of every human conscience as we attempt to change wicked hearts through speaking his powerful Word.

For these and other radical believers' wholesome addition to the freedom of individual human beings, to the peace of the world, and to the flourishing of human communities, I believe we should be thankful. However, I am most thankful that now Christians will rely on the only means God appointed from the church's beginning to propagate our beliefs: Faithful persuasion through loving proclamation. If we who are Christians will stay focused on proclaiming the good news about Jesus Christ, the Holy Spirit will do the rest through the prayers of God's people. May we never again forget the lessons these radical believers in Jesus once taught the other churches and the world.

Malcolm B. Yarnell III
Benbrook, Texas
October 14, 2023
(William Penn, advocate of liberty of conscience, was born this day in 1644)

The Five Points of a Baptist's Faith, Helwys Hall, Regents Park College, Oxford.

Introduction:
Religious Liberty—a Baptist Distinctive

On the wall of Helwys Hall at Regents Park College in Oxford, there is a five-pointed star, each point of which is inscribed with a Greek word. Translated into English, the words that label the star are "faith," "baptism," "fellowship," "freedom," and "evangelism." These were, according to Henry Wheeler Robinson, "The Five Points of a Baptist's Faith."[1] In other words, they represent the irreducible minimums that define and distinguish what it means to be "Baptist;" those vital distinctives that under-gird Baptist faith and practice and are intertwined to such a degree, that the absence or removal of any one of them produces an ecclesiastical system that can no longer be rightly referred to as "Baptist." To refer to these five words as "distinctives" is *not* to diminish the role any of these things may have had or do have in Christian traditions of different theological and ecclesiological persuasions; it *is* to note the vital and sometimes unique importance they are seen to play in an accurate portrayal of historic Baptist belief and behaviour. A study of historic Baptist documents—books, tracts, petitions, confessions of faith, and so forth—reveals the significance of these distinctives and the way they fit together.[2]

Baptists rejected the collapsing of the New Covenant into the Old functionally evident in paedobaptism, and so too the various state-church systems of various models of Christendom. Instead, holding personal responsibility and divine sovereignty in balance, they emphasised a salvation received by grace through *faith* in Christ: "believe on the Lord Jesus Christ and you will be saved" (Acts 16:31). Furthermore, according to the Baptists, only upon a person's profession of faith are they considered a suitable candidate for *baptism*—in other words, someone should not be baptised when they are born, but

---

[1] H. Wheeler Robinson, "The Five Points of a Baptist's Faith," *The Baptist Quarterly* 11, Nos. 1-2 (1942-1945): 4-14.

[2] For a collection of Baptist confessions with commentary, see William L. Lumpkin, *Baptist Confessions of Faith*, Second Revised Edition, ed. Bill J. Leonard (Valley Forge: Judson Press, 2011).

rather when they are "born again" with repentance and faith (John 3:1-15; Matt. 28:19; Acts 2:38).

Such baptism of believers ought to be done in the context of the *fellowship* of a local church, signifying unity with Christ and creating unity among Christians as the church is built up (1 Cor. 12:13; Gal. 3:26-28). True fellowship with Christ and among Christians is not created by coercion though, and no one should be forced in any way into the profession of any faith, the practise of any ritual, sacrament, or ordinance, adherence to any theological system, or membership in any religious institution. More specific to a Christian context, unbelievers should not be coerced to follow Christ, be baptised, or join a church since these are voluntary responses to the inward-working of the Holy Spirit through the preaching of the Scriptures.

This theological as opposed to humanistic approach to religious liberty, or *freedom* of conscience, is intrinsically linked to the Baptist "free church" ecclesiology whereby faith in Christ, not national heritage or religious parentage leads to baptism and fellowship. Furthermore, it historically fuelled Baptists' intentional evangelistic methodology. Because the weapons of our warfare are not of the flesh but of the Spirit (2 Cor. 10:4), and because we believe people become Christians not on the basis of governmental coercion, national citizenship, immediate family, or personal heritage, but as they hear the gospel and are called to repentance and faith in Jesus (Rom. 10:5-15), we devote ourselves to *evangelism*, proclaiming the good news of Jesus and making disciples to the ends of the earth (Matt. 28:18-20).

All of these points are worthy of in-depth exploration and detailed explanation. They remain historically significant and currently relevant. However, the present volume is primarily concerned with that of "freedom," in the sense of religious liberty.

When applied to specific aspects of modern-day life, the study of history is a powerful corrective to present confusion. The little volume you now hold is therefore born out of two primary motivations: I want people to know history and I want people to learn from history. More precisely in the case of this book, I want people to know and learn from *Baptist* history.

It is a travesty if members and even leaders of Baptist churches have a woefully deficient knowledge of the historical and theological formation of Baptist faith and practice, and yet this is all too often the case. Indeed, many baptistic believers seem to know more about—and hold greater respect for—people who would have at one time beheaded, burned, drowned, imprisoned, or tortured them than they do the very men and women of whom they are theological heirs and spiritual kin. A great deal of material has been written extolling the virtues and expounding the theologies of Luther, Zwingli, Calvin, Knox, and the Puritans but what of the lives and beliefs of those all-too-unknown Baptists who suffered many afflictions for the sake of their conscience and the consciences of others, the proclamation of the gospel, and the establishment of healthy churches pursuing a Christ-exalting submission to the authority of Scripture? As a Baptist pastor, I would like to see this tendency balanced out.

But this book is not only for those who would identify as "Baptist." Why should Baptists read and benefit from Anglican and Presbyterian history and literature, for example, but Anglicans, Presbyterians, and indeed anyone else not read and benefit from Baptist history and literature? Nonetheless, this book is not for the perpetuation of labels—helpful though they may be—but the promotion of liberty, a subject relevant to us all. Hopefully, its contents will be found useful to anyone committed to the continuation of biblical reformation and the growth of the church through the preaching of Christ.

Clearly identifying and expounding a historic, biblical theology of true religious freedom is a matter of particular importance for our present cultural moment. It should come as no surprise that there are many people in the world—whatever their beliefs—who do not have such freedom. Even Western readers unaccustomed to persecution of the variety those in the Global South experience would doubtless note a growing climate of anti-religious and especially anti-Christian antagonism. This hostility is fuelled by the influence of media and celebrity, and may in some cases even take legislative and judicial form, as public opinion shapes political orthodoxy and informs the actions of government and law enforcement officials, threatening liberty in a variety of ways, for people of different faiths. Non-conformity to the religious or irreligious *status quo* is at best frowned upon, and in many places suppressed—both legislatively and in far too many cases around the world, violently.

Even in the United States—a nation purportedly committed to the idea of "liberty and justice for all"—long enjoyed freedoms to believe and live accordingly are increasingly threatened by zealots across the political spectrum. Around the world, governmental overreach and the real or perceived suppression of freedoms by societal elites and influencers inevitably creates a reaction, but contemporary Populist push-back (of both left wing and right wing varieties) against "the establishment" often toes and eventually crosses the line of prejudice. Such prejudice is often not only religious but racialised: think at the most basic level of how some people view and speak about "Muslims" as though the word itself were obscene, or "Trojan Horse" hysteria that sees migration, asylum, and diaspora religio-cultural preservation as invasion, or the resurgence of Jew hatred in many forms, with far Right "Jews will not replace us" attitudes horseshoeing with the anti-Semetic theories and agendas of the radical Left, or the incorrect assumptions made about a person's beliefs and values based on audible and visual factors such as family name, language, accent, facial features, skin colour, clothing, and head-wear.

As Western society seems to push historic Christian faith and practice more and more back to its starting place at the margins of society, some embrace politicised systems such as Theonomy, Christian Reconstructionism, Dominionism, and Christian Nationalism, while others are less invested philosophically but still content with preserving and advancing a nominal, cultural Christianity. From young men listening to apologetics podcasts to old women attending praise and worship prayer rallies, from a black Pentecostal individual in Reading, England to a white evangelical mega-church in Redding, California, from the Kirk in Moscow, Idaho to the Kremlin in Moscow, Russia, these ideas increasingly hold sway. All manner of abusive attitudes, actions, strictures, and structures are sure to follow error—indeed, they have already done so, to great harm.

Under such circumstances, it is all the more important to remember those who have gone before us and dealt with similar issues in previous ages so that we can learn from them. We need to be able to say with our chests that Christ's Kingdom is not of this world, and that it is inappropriate to add his name or his people's identity as an appendage to a worldly political movement. We must catechise ourselves not to confuse divinely given roles and boundaries of authority, distorting the mission of God in Christ and his appointed means for kingdom advance in the church. We must reject worldly philosophies that produce systems and structures that result in persecution, religion by coercion not faith by conviction and conversion—and thereby an unregenerate church. And we must recognise the consequences, not least as seen across Europe, the United Kingdom, and North America: an under-evangelised and reactionary, rebellious society that remembers the abusive conduct of Christians, not the beauty and glory of Christ.

The prominent Baptist preacher of Victorian London, Charles Haddon Spurgeon, once said of Baptist Christians:

> The claim which we make to have been the first expositors and advocates in modern times of religious liberty, is based on the surest foundation, and is capable of the most satisfactory proof.[3]

The purpose of this volume is to examine that foundation, particularly within the historical and theological context of the years 1612–1689 and the cultural context of England. Hopefully readers will be both informed, and perhaps even transformed, by a better understanding of the early English Baptist development of a biblically distinctive theology of religious liberty in an era when it was not enjoyed by many and was endorsed by few, well before the radical cultural and intellectual shifts of the eighteenth century.

After introducing the historical setting and socio-religious context of the early English Baptists, representative contributions on the subject of religious liberty from early General and Particular Baptists will be explored—"General" and "Particular" referring to views of the extent of the atonement, and more broadly, distinguishing Calvinistic from non-Calvinist Baptists. It might be noted that not all are happy with the use of such categories, despite their prominent and consistent use in the relevant historiography.[4] Admittedly, such labels were not used at the time, and those later identified as "Baptist," were less concerned with labelling themselves and if they did, did so clumsily, choosing instead to express their identity in different ways, making themselves known more by their beliefs, practises, and associations than by names. The rejection of these categories is fairly recent and novel, and though intriguing—perhaps some may even find it compelling—not germane to the topic at hand: the doctrine of religious liberty as expressed by those in the soteriologically distinct but baptistic congregationalist traditions of, for example, the *Standard Confession* of 1660 ("General Baptists") and the *Confession of Faith* of 1677/1689 ("Particular Baptists").

While it is somewhat beyond the scope of the present volume to detail any implications history might have for a contemporary approach to religious liberty, I do hope these will be somewhat obvious and that this analysis of history and theology will provide an accessible framework for appropriate Christian engagement in response to apparent and emerging threats to religious liberty today, whether that liberty is our own or our neighbours'.

---

[3] C.H. Spurgeon, cited by Ian Randall, "Baptists, The Gospel and Freedom of Conscience," in *50th Anniversary Lecture of the SBHS* (Dunstable: Fauconberg Press, 2012), 15.

[4] Cf. Matthew C. Bingham, *Orthodox Radicals: Baptist Identity in the English Revolution* (Oxford: University Press, 2019).

Religious Liberty

At the centre of Helwys Hall's star of Baptist distinctives, is the Greek for "Lord Jesus." Ultimately, everything we believe and do must centre on Jesus Christ. The early English Baptist pursuit of universal religious liberty was not about liberty as an end in itself, but about the exaltation of Jesus as Lord. Because he is Lord, we must worship him regardless of restriction. Because he is Lord, we must proclaim him regardless of opposition. Because he is Lord, others must be allowed to live and worship in peace, with the Christian hope and mission being that they will hear and believe the gospel sincerely, without oppression. Because he is Lord, we believe that many will be persuaded by his message, amazed by his good news, and trust in and follow him.

Part One
The Crucible of Persecution[1]:
Surveying the Historical Context

---

[1] From a phrase used by Leon McBeth, *English Baptist Literature on Religious Liberty to 1689* (New York: Arno, 1980), 1.

Etch by Jan Luycken: **Burning of eight Anabaptists in Amsterdam, 1549**

1
Persecution of Continental Baptistic Movements[1]

Fairly early on in the days of the Protestant Reformation, some people began to leave Ulrich Zwingli's Zurich church after Zwingli gave the city council—instead of Scripture—authority in a matter of church practice. Through further Bible study, three men in particular—Felix Mantz, Conrad Grebel, and George Blaurock—came to believe in the institutional separation of church and state and a church membership comprised of believers at an age of understanding, baptised after personal profession of faith in Christ. These men and others in their group sought baptism as believers on January 25, 1525 and were soon called "Anabaptists"—a derogatory name meaning "rebaptisers" which came to be applied to several groups that practised believer's baptism and was generally rejected by those so-named.

"Anabaptist" teaching would spread quickly and on Easter Sunday 1525 we find a Roman Catholic priest named Balthasar Hubmaier baptising 300 believing parishioners.

These baptistic believers and their heirs made three particularly noteworthy contributions to reformation.

Ecclesiology—what the church is: The church is the assembly of people who truly believe their sins are removed by Christ, have been baptised as a confession of faith in him, and are committed to lives of reformation and repentance. The church is not an instrument of the state nor is the state an instrument of the church; they are separate. Church membership is then in no way connected to citizenship or parentage, but personal trust in Christ.

Ethics—what the church does: The Anabaptists were dismayed by how some were twisting the doctrine of justification by faith to excuse riotously sinful living, so emphasised "regeneration" instead of justification, and the changed life that true salvation brings. Their focus was less on the biblical teaching that

---

[1] For more on the subject of these movements, see Ian M. Randall, *Communities of Conviction: Baptist Beginnings in Europe* (Schwarzenfeld: Neufeld Verlag, 2009).

we are justified by faith apart from works, and more on the complementary teaching that true faith will produce good works that imitate Christ and are characterised by love.

Evangelism—how the church grows: The Reformation as led by Luther, Zwingli, and Calvin certainly had its missionaries, but is sometimes called "the Magisterial Reformation" because of its reliance on civil magistrates to legislate change and grow. The Anabaptists relied on God's Spirit changing people through the Scriptures, without the need for government support. They saw that true faith is not coerced and the church is not built through weapons of persecution but through patiently preaching the good news of God's word, so actively shared their faith with others.

After just a few years those who pioneered this movement for further reformation were dead: Grebel died in 1526 after imprisonment. Mantz was drowned in 1527. Hubmaier was burned in 1528 in Vienna and his wife Elisabeth was drowned in the Danube days later. Blaurock was burned in 1529.

The history of medieval Europe is often pervaded by gory tales of torture, hangings, burnings, and beheadings—and those who suffered these cruelties, like those who administered them, often did so because of their beliefs. The plight of the Anabaptists, who historically with the English Separatists preceded the Baptists,[2] is best summed up as "Catholics killed Protestants, Protestants killed Catholics, and they both agreed to kill Anabaptists."[3]

Consider the Continental Anabaptist Michael Sattler: in 1527 at the age of twenty-nine, he had his tongue torn out, before his tormentors lacerated his body with red-hot tongs and burned him alive. His wife was thrown into a river with a stone tied around her neck.[4] Tens of thousands were horrifically massacred all across the continent. Take Friesland, in the Netherlands, for example: from 1535-1546 no less than 30,000 baptistic believers[5] were put to death,

---

[2] James L. Garrett, *Baptist Theology* (Macon: Mercer University Press, 2009), 8-21.

[3] Tripp York, *The Purple Crown: the Politics of Martyrdom* (Scottdale, PA: Herald Press, 2007), cited by Brian Haymes, "'Thomas Helwys' The Mystery of Iniquity: Is it still relevant in the Twenty-First Century," in *Exploring Baptist Origins*, eds. Anthony R. Cross and Nicholas J. Wood (Oxford: Centre for Baptist History and Heritage, Regents Park College, 2010), 61.

[4] Erroll Hulse, *An Introduction to the Baptists* (Haywards Heath: Carey Publications, 1976), 18; cf. N. R. Needham, *2000 Years of Christ's Power, Part Three: Renaissance and Reformation* (London: Grace Publications Trust, 2004), 311-318.

[5] Reformation era sectarian observers of believers' baptism such as the evangelical Anabaptists, spiritual kinsmen of the modern Baptists who later sprang out of the English Separatists in the seventeenth century; cf. Hulse, *An Introduction*, 6.

by both Roman Catholics and Protestants. Like-minded believers in England were treated little differently.[6]

In short, "Christendom" was not Christ-like, nor was it friendly even to all who were professedly Christ-followers. It was not built around broad catholicity, or agreement on basic Christian beliefs and values, but specific scriptural interpretations, narrow personal preferences and quirks, and denominational distinctives. It was inherently inconsistent, made in the image of whoever was in control, and was often less about salvation and more about maintaining a spiritual and political *status quo,* power, the exaltation of nation-states or the advance of empires. Thus, Christians who contrasted the uniqueness of Christ's Kingdom with the Christo-tyrannies around them particularly suffered.

---

[6] Hulse, *An Introduction,* 19–20.

Benjamin Keach, pilloried for publishing a book of instruction for children that did not conform to the teachings of the Church of England

2
Persecution of the Early English Baptists

The English Separatist congregation in Gainsborough that would eventually move to London and become the first church to have the name "Baptist"[1] properly applied to it, was born out of persecution. Among the leading men within this congregation were John Smyth and Thomas Helwys. Smyth, a former Anglican priest, was prosecuted for "unlawfully preaching in public" in 1606.[2] Even the lawyer[3] Helwys did not escape persecution—his wife Joan was arrested.[4] These two men led a group to the Netherlands in 1608 to seek refuge from such harassment.[5]

After Helwys returned to England and planted a Baptist church in London in 1612, the Baptist movement began to expand. Since Baptist teaching constituted a threat both to the state and the church in the state-church system, they were persecuted—albeit not to the horrific extent of their English Protestant forbears and baptistic continental kinsmen. Due to a storm of public resentment, 1612 saw the last burnings for religious causes in England (of anti-Trinitarian heretics Bartholomew Legate and Edward Wightman).[6] But while such gruesome measures ceased and a superficially more tolerant spirit toward religious diversity developed among the Anglican laity, such attitudes were not extended by the civil or religious authorities and laws of the nation.[7]

A significant wave of persecution hit the fledgling Baptists in 1630, leading some of them to migrate to safer lands, while the activity of those remaining declined. This was followed in 1640 by a period of relative freedom, for Baptists at least, that extended through the civil wars and Oliver Cromwell's Protectorate, during which time Baptists were able to extensively and openly

---

[1] James L. Garrett, *Baptist Theology* (Macon: Mercer University Press, 2009), 23.
[2] Anthony R. Cross, "The Adoption of Believer's Baptism and Baptist Beginnings," in *Exploring Baptist Origins*, eds. Anthony R. Cross and Nicholas J. Wood (Oxford: Centre for Baptist History and Heritage, Regents Park College, 2010), 2.
[3] Cross, "The Adoption of Believer's Baptism," 2.
[4] Ian M. Randall, *Communities of Conviction: Baptist Beginnings in Europe* (Schwarzenfeld: Neufeld Verlag, 2009), 15.
[5] Garrett, *Baptist Theology*, 23.
[6] Leon McBeth, *English Baptist Literature on Religious Liberty to 1689* (New York: Arno, 1980), 11-12.
[7] McBeth, *English Baptist Literature*, 13-14.

preach and publish their beliefs, and enjoyed debating those beliefs with others with the assurance of greater security than previously enjoyed.[8] The religious liberty granted under the Protectorate was, however, somewhat specific to adherents of various strands of Protestant nonconformity, and the brutal subjugation of Catholics in Ireland and the Scottish Highlands carried not only political, but religious motivations. Bitter resentment for the sufferings inflicted and devastation caused remain to this day and can be a significant barrier to peaceful relations and gospel progress.

Upon the monarchy's restoration and the ascendency of Charles II to the throne, the government's program of persecuting Baptists (and others) resumed. One anonymously written document of the time details the government's campaign of terror against a few Baptist churches in London from 1661–1662:[9] while the churches were assembled, mercenary soldiers entered their meeting places on multiple occasions armed with swords and muskets. They frightened the women and children, smashed pulpits to pieces, broke down galleries, spoiled other goods throughout the meeting places, and violently assaulted members of the congregation. The perpetrators arrested some of the leading men in these churches, including the preacher, and held them for months without charge in prison, where the abuse continued at the hands of officials and fellow prisoners alike. Sometimes these and similar atrocities would be inflicted on the same congregations again during the evening meeting. The account includes the disturbing story of a one-year-old infant so frightened it became sick and died, and of a young boy wounded almost to death. It concludes with a gut-wrenching cry from the oppressed heart:

> Will not the stones in the street cry out (if we should hold our peace) against these wicked, filthy and Ungodly Proceedings of these Wicked men? and is it not the more to be lamented, that such things should be practiced in a Nation, who professe themselves to be Christians, and the only true Church separated from Rome? and yet they follow Romes steps in persecuting the Righteous, and all them of different Persuasions from them, and that they do so in such a way and manner by Violence,

---

[8] McBeth, *English Baptist Literature*, 8, 63.
[9] *Behold a cry! or, A true relation of the inhumane and violent outrages of divers souldiers, constables, and others, practised upon many of the Lord's people, commonly (though falsly) called Anabaptists at their several meetings in and about London* (London, 1662).

Cruelty, Spoile and Bloodshed, that Rome itself can hardly exceed them; and the very Heathen would be ashamed of them.[10]

Acute persecution lasted from 1660–1689, but the passing of the Act of Toleration in 1689 saw Baptists and other religious Non-conformist groups begin to benefit from a royally endorsed and enforced toleration for the first time.[11] True religious freedom was yet to be gained—Baptists, like Roman Catholics, Jews, and other religious minorities, were not allowed political office, for example —but the Act of Toleration allowed them to have their own places of worship and to appoint their own preachers and teachers. It was in this context of improved security for Non-conformist worship and witness that the work of Non-conformist ministerial training began to thrive, through the formation of "Dissenting Academies." These were, however, necessitated by and highlighted continuing social inequities, as the leading universities would not give places to non-Anglicans.

---

[10] *Behold a cry!* 9–10; When quoting directly from the original documents of primary sources, I have not attempted to update the spelling and punctuation of the original but record it throughout as it was written.

[11] Christopher Catherwood, *Church History: A Crash Course for the Curious* (Wheaton: Crossway Books, 2007), 152.

Miniature showing the expulsion of Jews following the Edict of Expulsion by Edward I of England (July 18, 1290)

3
Persecution of Non-Christians

Early English Baptists did not live in a bubble where everyone held certain Christian beliefs in common—the Trinity, or Christ's resurrection for example—but had just become unnecessarily violent over intramural conflicts. They were well aware of other religious minorities represented in the nation and around the world: from heretics who deviated from Christian orthodoxy to large world religions like Islam and Judaism. They were also aware that they were not unique in being persecuted, and that a consistent scripturally-informed and Christ-centred plea for religious liberty, pursuant of gospel clarity and church purity, must include their non-Christian neighbours.

These were days of increasing English commercial engagement with the Muslim world, in which adherents to Islam were honoured, but also feared and hated. The tensions went beyond mere religious prejudice. For example, the expansion of the Ottoman Empire into Europe during the reign of Süleyman the Magnificent (1520–1566) was of substantial geopolitical concern, and the bulk of the sixteenth and seventeenth centuries are bookended by Ottoman sieges of the great Habsburg city of Vienna. Meanwhile the Barbary pirates (Muslim raiders servicing the Ottoman slave trade) were building a reputation that would haunt coastal settlements from Iceland to West Africa and Mediterranean Europe for centuries. Richard Knolles reflected people's real and legitimate concerns when he wrote of the "the present terrour of the worlde" when recording his *General Historie of the Turkes* in 1603.[1]

Nonetheless, systemic abuses were inflicted upon everyday Muslim men and women who had little to do with Ottoman imperialism or Barbary slavery other than a shared religious identity and perhaps a common ethnicity. The reconquest of medieval Spain and Portugal from Muslim Moors of North African descent in 1492 (having begun over seven centuries before) gave way to

---

[1] Richard Knolles, *The Generall Historie of the Turkes, from the first beginning of that nation to the rising of the Othoman Familie: with all the notable expeditions of the Christian princes against them, together with the liues and conquests of the othoman kings and emperours faithfullie collected out of the best histories, both auntient and moderne, and digested into one continuat historie untill this present yeare 1603* (London: Adam Islip, 1603), 1.

forced conversions and baptisms into the Roman Catholic Church in the sixteenth century. Although modern social constructs of race and consequently racism had yet to be developed, there was an unmistakable racialised component to the sufferings inflicted on the Iberian Peninsula's Moorish families. This resulted in the seventeenth-century Moriscos ("Little Moors," those Moors who had through coercion, voluntarily, or by birth been brought into the Roman Catholic Church) being expelled, despite their conversion, from lands in which they and their families had lived for generations.[2]

England was a more tolerant environment for Muslims, most often simply called "Turks" or "Moors" at the time. Elizabeth's excommunication by the Roman Catholic Church left her and her kingdom ostracised from Europe not only theologically but commercially, forcing her to seek trade agreements and political alliances elsewhere. For her as a Protestant queen, the enemies (the Muslim world, not exactly united itself) of her enemy (Roman Catholic Europe), were her friends. Consequently, she established economically profitable and at times even personally warm relationships with the Sunni Ottoman Empire and Sa'di Sultanate, and the Shia Safavid Persian Empire, carrying on a particularly lengthy correspondence with the Ottoman Sultan Murad III.[3]

Of course, England was not without its prejudices. Doubtless there were Muslims who fell afoul of Elizabeth I's anxieties about the growing black population. In an open letter to the Lord Mayor of London, Elizabeth explained in 1596 that "there are of late divers blackmoores brought into this realme, of which kinde of people there are already here to manae."[4] A week later, she expressed her "good pleasure to have those kinde of people sent out of the lande."[5] No legal action was taken, so a few years later in 1601, Elizabeth argued (again unsuccessfully) for the deportation of "the great number of Negars and Blackamoors which (as she is informed) are crept into this realm."[6] Never mind, of course, the English merchants, privateers, and the

---

[2] For a study of this, see Matthew Carr, *Blood and faith: the purging of Muslim Spain, 1492-1614* (London: Hurst & Company, 2017).

[3] For a study of Elizabethan-Islamic relations, see Jerry Brotton, *This Orient Isle: Elizabethan England and the Islamic World* (London: Allen Lane, 2016); also Gerald M. MacLean and Nabil Matar eds., *Britain and the Islamic World, 1558-1713* (Oxford: Oxford University Press, 2011).

[4] John Roche Dasent, ed., *Acts of the Privy Council of England*, n.s., vol. 26, 1596-1597 (London: Macklemore, 1902), 16-17.

[5] Dasent, *"Acts of the Privy Council,"* 20-21.

[6] Paul L. Hughes and James F. Larkin eds., "Licensing Casper van Senden to Deport Negroes [draft]. Ca. January 1601," in *Tudor Royal Proclamations, Vol. 3, The Later Tudors (1588-1603)* (New Haven/London: Yale University Press, 1969), 221-222.

like who were themselves creeping into other realms that England would soon invade and exploit.

Elizabeth's xenophobia on these occasions was more with regard to race not religious affiliation, and the majority of her targets were pagan not Muslim, but it demonstrates the limits to her tolerance when there was less apparent benefit or when a bargaining chip was needed.[7] Elizabeth attempted to give her prejudice spiritual credibility by appealing to a sense of Christian Nationalism, condemning these people for "having no understanding of Christ or his Gospel." Of course, Elizabeth's prejudiced attitude and words were in fact at variance with Christ and his gospel, and had they been acted upon would have if anything pushed people away: spiritually from wanting to consider the gospel message, and geographically from ready access to those willing to share it.

While substantial enough for there to be voluntary religious conversions from and to Islam in sixteenth and seventeenth-century England, the settled Muslim presence remained quite small. Would sentiment have changed with more obvious population growth? It is impossible to say with complete certainty, but historical precedent would suggest that is likely. In any case, relations cooled after Elizabeth's reign. Throughout the seventeenth century Muslims remained (as was still the case under Elizabeth I) very much outsiders and the subjects of stereotype, tolerated at times for economic reasons and cultural curiosity, but not entirely welcome or at liberty—just more-so than in Roman Catholic Continental Europe.

The Jews, however, do not seem to have been welcome to any degree anywhere—and England was no exception. For centuries, Jews had no legal standing whatsoever in the British Isles, after they were expelled on July 18, 1290 by King Edward I. Their lived experience prior to that date was defined by consistent suspicion, stigma, economic oppression, persecution, and a relentlessly hostile environment, particularly in the twelfth and thirteenth centuries. Jews were massacred in England itself, and as though that were not quite enough, by English Crusaders marauding their way to the Middle East. Jews were victims of blood libels—that is, accusations (which endure, in various forms, to this day) that they ritually murdered Christian boys and used their blood in

---

[7] Cf. Emily C. Bartels, "Too Many Blackamoors: Deportation, Discrimination, and Elizabeth I," *Studies in English Literature, 1500-1900*, 46, No. 2 (Spring 2006): 305-322; Emily Weissbourd, "'Those in Their Possession': Race, Slavery, and Queen Elizabeth's 'Edicts of Expulsion,'" *Huntington Library Quarterly* 78, No. 1 (Spring 2015): 1-19.

their rituals, particularly in the preparation of Passover matzah—which resulted in Populist uprisings and violence. They were subjected to anti-Jewish prejudice at a personal level, and to institutionalised anti-Judaism. In 1218, English Jews were ordered to wear on their outer garments an identification badge showing the stone tablets of Mt. Sinai, and this was reinforced in 1253.[8] In 1222, they were forbidden from building new synagogues. Before the national expulsion of 1290, they endured localised expulsion and increasing marginalisation. For example, in 1271, a group of Friars from a local monastery made a noise complaint to the king of "great howlings" the Jews made in their worship. The synagogue was subsequently seized—and given, conveniently, to the Friars.[9]

After King Edward I expelled all Jews from England by decree on July 18, 1290, England's Jews had just over three months to leave, taking only what they could carry. Anything they left behind was seized by the king, who enriched himself with the plunder. Many lost not only their livelihoods but their very lives as they fled. It would be almost four centuries before their descendants could legally return. Some evaded expulsion by pretending to be Christians. However, the sincerity of these conversions is difficult to assess considering the climate of coerced religion leading to conversion because it seemed expedient, not because the convert was spiritually regenerate.[10]

In Spain, even willing Jewish converts to Christianity fell under suspicion—they were in fact the main targets of the Spanish Inquisition, along with others found to secretly continue the practice of Jewish faith. Prior to any legal reversal of Edward I's expulsion order or effort at resettlement, refugees from this persecuted Spanish community, called "Conversos" or "New Christians," came to the United Kingdom over the course of the sixteenth-century. Those who secretly continued to practise the Jewish faith did so at risk of exposure and deportation. Most notably, Dr. Rodrigo Lopez, a Jewish convert, was accused of conspiring with Spain to poison the queen. He maintained both

---

[8] John V. Tolan, "The first imposition of a badge on European Jews: the English royal mandate of 1218," in *The Character of Christian-Muslim Encounter: Essays in honour of David Thomas*, eds. Douglas Pratt, Jon Hoover, John Davies, and John A. Chesworth (Netherlands: Brill, 2016), 145-146.

[9] Henry Thomas, *The Ancient Remains, Antiquities, and Recent Improvements, of the City of London... Vol. 2* (London: Sears, 1830), 12.

[10] For more on persecution of Jews see Birgit Weidl, "Anti-Jewish legislation in the Middle Ages" in *Comprehending Antisemitism through the Ages: A Historical Perspective*, eds. Armin Lange, Kerstin Mayerhofer, Dina Porat, and Lawrence H. Schiffman (Boston: DeGruyter, 2021), 183-215.

his innocence and his sincere Christian faith, but his Jewish background was weaponised in the accusation. He was hung, drawn, and quartered in 1594, sending any who may have been minded to practise their Jewish faith more openly back into secrecy.[11]

It was into such a world of religious coercion and persecution that a numerically small and socially suppressed group of Baptist believers pleaded for religious liberty, not only for themselves but for anyone who could be called their neighbour.[12]

---

[11] João Vicente Melo, "Roderigo Lopez (c.1525-1594)," in *Lives in Transit in Early Modern England: Identity and Belonging*, ed. Nandini Das (Amsterdam: University Press, 2022), 157–164.

[12] Leon McBeth, *English Baptist Literature on Religious Liberty to 1689* (New York: Arno, 1980), 1.

Part Two
Preaching, Not Persecuting[1]:
Early General Baptists

---

[1] From a phrase used by Leonard Busher, in L. Busher, "Religion's Peace: A Plea for Liberty of Conscience," in *Tracts on Liberty of Conscience and Persecution 1614-1661*, ed. Edward B. Underhill (London: J. Haddon, 1846), 32.

John Smyth (1554–1612)

4
John Smyth

It is a false dichotomy to ask if the Baptists derived their theology from Anabaptism *or* English Separatism, and it is agenda-driven historical revisionism to deny the role those called "Anabaptists" played in early Baptist history, although they were indeed a distinct group.[1] It might be better to say that the Baptists came *from* English Separatism *through* the influence of what was called Anabaptism. After the Gainsborough congregation led by John Smyth and Thomas Helwys arrived in Holland, they became influenced by "Anabaptist" teaching, particularly with regard to their view of believer's baptism. In either 1608 or 1609, Smyth, acting upon the congregation's authority and in its presence, baptised himself and those who were with him, and constituted a church.[2]

It was not long, however, before Smyth was having second thoughts about baptising himself, and so fearing the illegitimacy of his act, he led thirty-one members of the Gainsborough group in applying for baptism and membership with the Waterlander Mennonites (Mennonites were one of the continent's evangelical Radical Reformation movements called "Anabaptists").[3] The process was lengthy, and Smyth died in 1612, before his congregation was accepted by the Mennonites in 1615.[4]

Smyth's spiritual journey took him through Puritan, Separatist, and baptistic schools of thought.[5] With his developing theology came changes in the way he thought about the relationship between church and state. In 1607, while still a Separatist, he was of the belief that civil magistrates should "abolish

---

[1] Con. Chris Traffanstedt, "A Primer on Baptist History: The True Baptist Trail," *The Reformed Reader*, November 16, 2022, http://www.reformedreader.org/history/pbh.htm.

[2] Anthony R. Cross, "The Adoption of Believer's Baptism and Baptist Beginnings," in *Exploring Baptist Origins*, eds. Anthony R. Cross and Nicholas J. Wood (Oxford: Centre for Baptist History and Heritage, Regents Park College, 2010), 8.

[3] Ian M. Randall, *Communities of Conviction: Baptist Beginnings in Europe* (Schwarzenfeld: Neufeld Verlag, 2009), 19.

[4] James L. Garrett, *Baptist Theology* (Macon: Mercer University Press, 2009), 23.

[5] Slayden A. Yarbrough, "The English Separatist Influence on the Baptist Tradition of Church-State Issues," *Baptist History and Heritage* 20, No. 3 (July, 1985): 21.

idolatry and all false ways."[6] The Separatists detached themselves from the Church of England because they were opposed to the Puritan approach to reformation, which was to remain in the corrupt and compromised church and wait for the civil authorities to enforce the needed changes.[7] Nevertheless, the breakaways had much in common with those they were leaving: the Separatists, like the Puritans, held primarily to a religious liberty that benefited themselves, served their interests, and advanced their agenda: a liberty for me, but not for thee. They believed that theologically errant authorities should stop persecuting those who uphold the truth, but were quite happy for the tables to be turned, especially as they perceived themselves to be upholders of truth. This subjective mindset meant that the religious freedom they desired amounted, logically, to their liberty to deny others liberty.[8] It was not dissimilar from the Magisterial Reformers' understanding, which was "sporadic and expedient" and "applied only to those with correct doctrine."[9] The boundaries of what constituted "correct doctrine" were liable to change with shifts in power, but the principle that people could uphold "correct doctrine" by force and persecution remained in place, even to the destruction of its former practitioners. The self-destructive potential of such a policy is illustrated in the stories of the Archbishop of Canterbury Thomas Cranmer and Bishop of London Nicholas Ridley in the sixteenth-century, under whose authority religious Non-conformists were burned at the stake. When the balance of power eventually shifted, they themselves were burned at the stake.

In 1612 (whether before or after Smyth's death is disputed),[10] a confession was issued entitled *Propositions and Conclusions concerning the True Christian Religion, containing a Confession of faith of certain English people, living at Amsterdam*. At the very least it was based on a draft written by Smyth.[11] The confession is likely the first Christian confession of faith to develop a statement

---

[6] Randall, *Communities of Conviction*, 6.

[7] Yarbrough, "The English Separatist Influence," 21.

[8] Leon McBeth, *English Baptist Literature on Religious Liberty to 1689* (New York: Arno, 1980), 14-15; Barrie White, "Early Baptist Arguments for Religious Freedom: Their Overlooked Agenda," *Baptist History and Heritage* 24, No. 4 (October, 1989): 3.

[9] Malcolm B. Yarnell III, "The Development of Religious Liberty: A Survey of its Progress and Challenges in Christian History," *Journal for Baptist Theology and Ministry* 6, No. 1 (Spring 2009): 131.

[10] Garrett, *Baptist Theology*, 29.

[11] Paul S. Fiddes, "Church and Sect: Cross-Currents in Early Baptist Life," in *Exploring Baptist Origins*, eds. Anthony R. Cross and Nicholas J. Wood (Oxford: Regent's Park College, 2010), 45.

promoting religious liberty.[12] Article 84 is the first claim on religious liberty in the English language. The article declares

> That the magistrate is not by virtue of his office to meddle with religion, or matters of conscience, to force or compel men to this or that form of religion, or doctrine: but to leave Christian religion free, to every man's conscience, and to handle only civil transgressions ... injuries and wrongs of man against man, in murder, adultery, theft, etc., for Christ only is the king, and lawgiver of the church and conscience.[13]

The Smyth confession certainly states that there should be freedom for all who would be labelled as "Christians,"[14] but, strong as the statement is, it is not so clear on the matter of *universal* religious freedom: the right of people to believe and practise belief as they please without persecution or governmental harassment. He only writes "leave Christian religion free," which might indicate that governmental interference in other religions is acceptable. That said, the limitations placed on civil magistrates (they are not "to meddle with religion, or matters of conscience, to force or compel men to this or that form of religion, or doctrine"), if the article were to be implemented, would seem to result in the universal liberty more explicitly argued for by later Baptists. The theological foundation that "Christ only is the king" in matters of church and conscience also leads logically to a position of universal liberty, as it deprives civil authorities of the power to intervene in a person's faith.

While not as unequivocal as perhaps it could be, Smyth's statement was a radical development. The majority of theologians historically had denied religious liberty.[15] Certainly the Roman Catholic Church with its Crusades and Inquisitions was not known at that point in its history for liberty or even a milder toleration. The Magisterial Reformers were little different at this point—although they seem at times perhaps to have been more restrained. Luther, Calvin, Zwingli, and their theological forbear Augustine all supported some form of religious coercion and persecution—even to death. In need of biblical warrant, they relied primarily on selected, somewhat out of context,

---

[12] Garrett, *Baptist Theology*, 31.
[13] *Propositions and Conclusions concerning the True Christian Religion, containing a Confession of faith of certain English people, living at Amsterdam* (1612).
[14] Yarbrough, "The English Separatist Influence," 21.
[15] Yarnell, "Religious Liberty," 119.

John Smyth

Old Testament passages to justify their position. No attempt was made to interpret these texts through a Christological, New Testament lens and conversely, when New Testament texts were examined on this subject, it was through an Old Testament lens.[16]

Smyth's stint as a Separatist no doubt contributed in an important way to his idea of religious liberty: Separatist beliefs in a voluntary church membership and a congregationally appointed leadership set them apart from other reformation traditions, such as the Erastian model of Lutheranism and the English Reformation—where the state had authority over the church to make decisions related to the church. That said, the Separatists were not quite as detached from the Reformed model of Zwingli and Calvin, where the church retained some authority over the state.[17] It appears that while Smyth's views were still transitioning at the time of his death, he was moving away from this to what would become the standard Baptist position. His final progression to a more universal understanding of religious liberty was not so much due to Separatist influence, but to that of the Anabaptists. Indeed, Smyth's acceptance along with his followers of believers' baptism may be seen as a turning point: accepting a person's freedom to accountably profess *personal* faith in Christ and to express that by passing through the waters of baptism as a believer was logically inseparable from belief in liberty of conscience in a context where the expectation was baptism upon birth into the belief dictated by the state and surrounding society.[18]

---

[16] There appears almost to be a "presupposition that neither testament may be interpreted Christologically." Yarnell, "Religious Liberty," 120; cf. 119-122; 127-129.

[17] Yarbrough, "The English Separatist Influence," 14.

[18] Randall, *Communities of Conviction*, 6-7.

Message to King James I by Thomas Helwys in his book A Short Declaration of the Mistery of Iniquity (1612), that resulted in Helwys' imprisonment and death

5
Thomas Helwys

When Smyth began to believe that he and his congregation should have been baptised by the Mennonites, Thomas Helwys disagreed and with around ten others, separated from the original group.[1] Following this split, Helwys and his followers returned to England, where they established what most historians agree to be the first "Baptist" (as opposed to simply baptistic) church in the country at Pinners Hall, Spitalfields, London in 1612.[2] The same year, Helwys published *A Short Declaration of the Mistery of Iniquity* and addressed it to King James I. Although it may not be well-arranged, is repetitious, and contains allusions without explanations,[3] this unquestionably bold and brave work represents a passionate plea for universal religious freedom,[4] giving it its best defence England had seen up until that time.[5] It may well have been written with the tone "of a deeply loyal subject speaking a prophetic word to a Godly Prince,"[6] but living in days of persecution in a country with a church established by the state, endorsed by the state, enforced by the state, and ruled by

---

[1] Brian Haymes, "'Thomas Helwys' *The Mystery of Iniquity*: Is it still relevant in the Twenty-First Century,*" in *Exploring Baptist Origins*, eds. Anthony R. Cross and Nicholas J. Wood (Oxford: Centre for Baptist History and Heritage, Regents Park College, 2010), 63.

[2] Erroll Hulse, *An Introduction to the Baptists* (Haywards Heath: Carey Publications, 1976), 18; cf. N. R. Needham, *2000 Years of Christ's Power, Part Three: Renaissance and Reformation* (London: Grace Publications Trust, 2004), 25; Haymes, "Thomas Helwys," 64; F. L. Cross, "Helwys, Thomas," in *The Oxford Dictionary of the Christian Church*, 3rd. rev. ed, ed. E. A. Livingstone (Oxford: University Press, 2005), 753; Augustus Charles Bickley, "Helwys, Thomas," in *Dictionary of National Biography, Vol. 25, Harris—Henry I.*, eds. Leslie Stephen and Sidney Lee (New York: Macmillan and Co., 1891), 375.

[3] Leon McBeth, *English Baptist Literature on Religious Liberty to 1689* (New York: Arno, 1980), 30.

[4] Anthony R. Cross, "The Adoption of Believer's Baptism and Baptist Beginnings," in *Exploring Baptist Origins*, eds. Anthony R. Cross and Nicholas J. Wood (Oxford: Centre for Baptist History and Heritage, Regents Park College, 2010), 28; James L. Garrett, *Baptist Theology* (Macon: Mercer University Press, 2009), 33; Haymes, "Thomas Helwys," 65; McBeth, *English Baptist Literature*, 30.

[5] Ian M. Randall, *Communities of Conviction: Baptist Beginnings in Europe* (Schwarzenfeld: Neufeld Verlag, 2009), 23.

[6] Paul S. Fiddes, "Church and Sect: Cross-Currents in Early Baptist Life," in *Exploring Baptist Origins*, eds. Anthony R. Cross and Nicholas J. Wood (Oxford: Regent's Park College, 2010), 52–53.

the head of state, Helwys was treading on dangerous ground. King James had on several occasions expressed his displeasure with religious persecution, but he was concerned to keep order, and for him order meant uniformity. Any voices of dissent would continue to be punished.[7]

Helwys wished a happy and prosperous reign to King James, and offered a word of prayer that wisdom would be granted to him to righteously rule and judge the people of Great Britain. But he drew a distinction between King James on "the princely throne of that mighty kingdom of Great Britain" and "our Lord Jesus Christ in power and majesty ... upon David's throne, the throne of the kingdom of Israel, which his Father has given unto him."[8] This separation of the world's kings and Heaven's King, a "two spheres" approach to church and state with two distinct swords of authority (secular and ecclesiastical), is foundational to *A Short Declaration*'s direct plea for religious liberty itself. This separation, where Christ governs the church and the king governs the secular society, clashed with the philosophy expressed in the Book of Common Prayer (1562):

> BEING by God's Ordinance, according to Our just Title, Defender of the Faith, and Supreme Governor of the Church, within these Our Dominions, We hold it most agreeable to this Our Kingly Office, and Our own religious Zeal, to conserve and maintain the Church committed to Our Charge, in Unity of true Religion, and in the Bond of Peace; and not to suffer unnecessary Disputations, Altercations, or Questions to be raised, which may nourish Faction both in the Church and Commonwealth.[9]

Helwys clearly spells out the implications his proposed separation bears for the role of civil authorities as concerns religion:

> And if the king's people be obedient and true subjects, obeying all human laws made by the king, our lord the king can require no more. For men's religion to God is between God and themselves. The king shall not answer for it. Neither may the king be judge between God and man. Let them be heretics, Turks, Jews, or whatsoever, it appertains not to the earthly power to punish them in the least measure.[10]

---

[7] McBeth, *English Baptist Literature*, 6.
[8] Haymes, "Thomas Helwys," 69.
[9] McBeth, *English Baptist Literature*, 7.
[10] Haymes, "Thomas Helwys," 70.

If the king were of the opinion that he could preside over the spiritual lives of his subjects, Helwys makes clear that this would be to take the position of the immortal God and not mortal man.[11] He also highlights how ineffectual compulsion of religion is for eternity and the judgement, though to give in to government demands may make life on Earth more peaceful:

> Oh let the king be judge, is it not most equal that men should choose their religion themselves, seeing they only must stand before the judgement seat of God to answer for themselves, when it shall be no excuse for them to say we were commanded or compelled to be of this religion by the king or by them that had authority from him.[12]

Such a philosophy may be taken for granted by many (not all!) today, particularly in the West, but it was somewhat revolutionary in Helwys' day. It seems likely that this perspective on religious liberty, more developed than Smyth's, owes much to the influence of the "Anabaptists" with whom the Gainsborough group were in contact in the Netherlands. While the various groups called Anabaptists may have largely operated in "survival mode" and tended towards socio-political isolation in a hostile society,[13] the Anabaptist theologian and former Roman Catholic priest Balthasar Hubmaier had written on religious liberty as early as 1524 in *On Heretics and Those who Burn Them*. Defining heretics as those who "wantonly resist the Holy Scripture" and distort its meaning, Hubmaier wrote "those who are such should be overcome with holy instruction, not contentiously but gently,"[14] and if they are not overcome and do not yield to such instruction "then avoid them and let them go on to rant and rage (Titus 3:10)." Hubmaier was tortured on the rack in Vienna and burned alive as one of the "heretics" whose lives he had written to save, but his work lived on and many of the same basic arguments outlined by Hubmaier were later developed and expounded by Baptists of both General and Particular theological streams.

---

[11] McBeth, *English Baptist Literature*, 31.
[12] Haymes, "Thomas Helwys," 74.
[13] Slayden A. Yarbrough, "The English Separatist Influence on the Baptist Tradition of Church-State Issues," *Baptist History and Heritage*, 20, No. 3 (July, 1985), 14.
[14] Balthasar Hubmaier, "On Heretics and Those who Burn Them", in *Balthasar Hubmaier: Theologian of Anabaptism*, trans., eds. H. Wayne Pipkin and John Howard Yoder (Scottdale: Herald Press, 1989), 59-66.

Helwys suffered as well. What may seem to us to be a reasonable and just call for religious liberty and freedom of conscience was considered inappropriate and highly dangerous. Helwys was subsequently arrested, in all probability because of the views set forth in *Mistery of iniquity*, and died in 1615 or 1616, apparently still in Newgate Prison.[15] Though dead, he continued to speak through his successors.

---

[15] Randall, *Communities of Conviction*, 25.

Portrait of James I (1566–1625), King of England, Anonymous, 1614

6
Leonard Busher

Little is known about Leonard Busher; indeed it is conjecture that leads us to think he was a member of the London church led by Helwys.[1] We do know that his work went further than that of Helwys and he wrote the first work devoted *exclusively* to religious liberty in the English language.[2] *Religions Peace: A Plea for Liberty of Conscience* (1614) may be the only extant document that bears Busher's name, but within its pages, this early English Baptist effectively completed laying the foundations already begun by Smyth and Helwys.

Early on, Busher deals with one of the underlying issues connected with religious coercion and persecution. A consistent Erastian ecclesiology that produces a "national" or "state" church fails to properly distinguish between citizens and church members, those who have been born into a country, and those who have been re-born into Christ. No one, Busher argues, whether they belong to the nobility or the common folk, can have true religion's reverential relationship with God by being physically born—a person must be spiritually born again with repentance toward God and faith in the Lord Jesus Christ (John 3:3).[3] This regeneration comes "by the word preached only," for the word is the sword of the Holy Spirit.[4] The practical implications of this for a monarch, particularly one who professed to be a Christian, are clearly spelled out:

> let it please your majesty and parliament to be entreated to revoke and repeal those antichristian, Romish, and cruel laws, that force all in our land, both prince and people to receive that religion wherein the king or queen were born, or that which is established by the law of man. And instead thereof, enact and publish that apostolic, Christian, gentle, and

---

[1] L. Busher, "Religion's Peace: A Plea for Liberty of Conscience," in *Tracts on Liberty of Conscience and Persecution 1614-1661*, ed. Edward B. Underhill (London: J. Haddon, 1846), 5.

[2] Leon McBeth, *English Baptist Literature on Religious Liberty to 1689* (New York: Arno, 1980), 39.

[3] Busher, "Religion's Peace," 5; McBeth, *English Baptist Literature*, 42.

[4] Busher, "Religion's Peace," 16.

merciful law of Christ—viz. Go, teach all nations, preach the gospel to every creature.[5]

For Busher then, removing laws of religious coercion would establish liberty, but should not (as some likely feared) remove faith from the public square. Quite the contrary! It would result in greater openness and increased intelligent discussion about faith. A Christian can and should defend the faith, but even as faith comes only by the word and Spirit of God, so it is only by these things that it should be defended.[6] The fundamental two swords/spheres doctrine is restated, with the injunction that those who rule temporal affairs and those who rule spiritual affairs are "not to meddle one with another's authority, office, and function."[7] To behave otherwise is to force the conscience and thus spiritually rape the nation's citizens.[8] The land is not thereby filled with people of true faith, but rather with hypocrites.[9]

Busher is not only concerned with the purity of people's faith, but also with that of princes' (civil and ecclesiastical) minds. Professedly Christian rulers who compel people into falsely saying that they believe, who "force men to church against their consciences,"[10] and who seek to establish Christ's Kingdom with the weapons of this world[11] are not thinking as Christ thought. In Busher's own words

> Persecution is a work well pleasing to all false prophets and bishops, but it is contrary to the mind of Christ "who came not to judge and destroy men's lives, but to save them."[12]

Busher is unequivocal: any who persecute cannot claim to have the liberty of the gospel. This liberty is found in the love of Christ and is demonstrated by the Christian's love for others as the gospel is proclaimed, not as people are forced to church, deported, imprisoned, tortured, drowned, burned, hanged, or beheaded. Those guilty of such persecutory behaviour neglect to walk

---

[5] Busher, "Religion's Peace," 16.
[6] McBeth, *English Baptist Literature*, 42.
[7] Busher, "Religion's Peace," 23.
[8] Busher, "Religion's Peace," 34.
[9] Busher, "Religion's Peace," 29–30.
[10] Busher, "Religion's Peace," 18.
[11] Busher, "Religion's Peace," 19.
[12] Busher, "Religion's Peace," 17, 27.

wisely toward outsiders (Col. 4:1) and create a major stumbling block by needlessly offending "the Jews and all other strangers, who account it tyranny to have their consciences forced to religion by persecution."[13] Not only does this hurt gospel witness toward such groups, but "Thereby are the Jews, Turks, and Pagans occasioned and encouraged to persecute likewise all such as preach and teach Christ in their dominions."[14] The only area where persecution succeeds is in the destruction of lost souls, who from a strictly human, earthbound perspective, might have come to repentance and faith had they been allowed to live.[15] Again, persecution is not in line with the mind of Christ: "The Lord wills not that the believing should live to the destruction of the unbelieving, but unto their conversion, edification, and salvation."[16]

For Busher, there really is very little difference between the Church of England and the Church of Rome, especially when it comes to the methods used to increase membership.[17] Reproduction, not spiritual regeneration, keeps their membership sustainable. In order to retain authority over those born into the church, Busher accuses the bishops of suppressing the critical pursuit of knowledge and disabling people from fulfilling 1 John 4:1, which tells people to examine "the spirits" to see if they are of God—an impossibility,

> except they hear and read other men's doctrines as well as the bishops' and their ministers'. Neither can they if they would, so long as the bishops have power from the king and state to silence and imprison, &c., all preachers, and to burn all books which teach not their doctrines.[18]

He might well have quoted Hubmaier at this point: "To burn innocent paper is a trifle, but to demonstrate what is error and to prove the same with Scripture is an art."[19]

Although Busher's appeal for freedom does cover people of all beliefs and not just his own,[20] his context necessitated that he plea particularly for professing Christians who are in some way detached from the established church.

---

[13] Busher, "Religion's Peace," 28.
[14] Busher, "Religion's Peace," 33.
[15] Busher, "Religion's Peace," 17, 28.
[16] Busher, "Religion's Peace," 21.
[17] Busher, "Religion's Peace," 19.
[18] Busher, "Religion's Peace," 20.
[19] Balthasar Hubmaier, "On Heretics and Those who Burn Them," in *Balthasar Hubmaier: Theologian of Anabaptism*, trans., eds. H. Wayne Pipkin and John Howard Yoder (Scottdale: Herald Press, 1989), 65.
[20] McBeth, *English Baptist Literature*, 47.

Busher writes that those responsible for persecution place themselves in the same category as Cain, Ishmael, and Esau, "figures of all persecutors who are not representatives of the true church."[21] There is also the danger, he argues, that by persecuting anyone who doesn't go along with the status quo, the civil authorities run the risk of persecuting to death "true ambassadors of the Lord" (Busher here draws on Jesus' parable of the tares—Matthew 13:24–30, 36–43).[22]

Busher unfavourably contrasts the current practice of professing Christians in England with that of Muslims in Constantinople, a contrast that along with his earlier comparison of the Church of England to the Church of Rome, demonstrates shrewd knowledge of politicians and their thought processes. Supporting his argument that the Turks allowed greater liberty by both anecdote and evidence, Busher asks:

> If this be so, how much more ought Christians not to force one another to religion? And how much more ought Christians to tolerate Christians, when as the Turks do tolerate them? Shall we be less merciful than the Turks? Or shall we learn the Turks to persecute the Christians? It is not only unmerciful, but unnatural and abominable; yea, monstrous for one Christian to vex and destroy another for difference and questions of religion.[23]

According to Busher, it is a far greater tyranny for a Christian in civil authority to persecute fellow Christians, than it is for a pagan to persecute them. It might come as no surprise for a pagan government to behave in such a way, but Christians ought to have greater knowledge and should show more mercy.[24]

While Busher's religious liberty is universal, it is not utopian or absolute.[25] He is aware that there will be those who attempt to take advantage of their liberty in order to usurp that of others. "The king and parliament may please to permit all sorts of Christians; yea, Jews, Turks, and pagans," he writes, with the caveat "so long as they are peaceable, and no malefactors."[26] His vision

---

[21] Busher, "Religion's Peace," 21.
[22] Busher, "Religion's Peace," 24–25, 27.
[23] Busher, "Religion's Peace," 24; cf. Barrie White, "Early Baptist Arguments for Religious Freedom: Their Overlooked Agenda," *Baptist History and Heritage* 24, No. 4 (October, 1989): 6.
[24] Busher, "Religion's Peace," 36.
[25] White, "Early Baptist Arguments," 7–8.
[26] Busher, "Religion's Peace," 33.

for religious liberty certainly did not entail going soft on law-enforcement or turning a blind eye to extremists! Nor did it require acceptance of religious practices that result in violations of the second table of the Ten Commandments—murder for example. Traitors to Crown and country were to be strongly penalised *irrespective* of religious affiliation and Busher makes some suggestions as to appropriate penalties. It might seem that the difference between Busher and King James hinges simply on the definition of "traitor". For Busher, traitors are all those who, irrespective of religion, are *actually guilty* of plotting or causing real civil unrest resulting in actual harm, while for James traitors were those who might *possibly* have the potential to plot and cause civil unrest, generally singled out as such for non-conforming (Christian and otherwise) religious affiliations—such as, in James' Britain, Baptists or Roman Catholics. By James' definition, merely preaching Baptist theology was an imprisonable offence, while Busher had other activities altogether in mind. The definition of this one word makes a world of difference.

Busher's religious liberty is not simply a freedom to worship, where religious adherents are confined to their own pre-existing circles and prohibited from proselytising. People should be free to write for or against anything concerning any matter of religion, but ideally this should be done with fairness: Scripture should be *the* authority when Christians are discussing Scripture and participants in such debates should not slander each other.[27] None of these restrictions are sufficient to keep Busher from strongly denouncing false teaching, particularly that of the "anti-Christian" Roman Catholic Church:

> Through the continuance whereof, not only the apostolic church is continued still in the wilderness and desert of this world; but also the Jews and others, both in Great Britain and all over the world, are kept back from the knowledge of God's holy word, the only order and ordinance Christ hath appointed for the gathering of his church together, out of all places of the world.[28]

While urging Christians to exercise wisdom and caution in dealing with those who have placed themselves under the authority of the papacy, Busher's

---

[27] Busher, "Religion's Peace," 33.
[28] Busher, "Religion's Peace," 47.

faith is in the power of the preached word—not the fire and sword of civil authorities—to punish and ultimately destroy those he believes have the spirit of antichrist. Allowing religious liberty will hasten that day:

> Let them enjoy freedom of the gospel and liberty of conscience: that so the apostolic church, which is scattered and driven into the wilderness and desert of this world, may be again gathered together, both Jews and Gentiles, into visible and established congregations and that the catholic and universal church of antichrist may be consumed and abolished, by his word and Spirit, as the holy apostle hath foretold.[29]

Not only would society be free to discern, but by using this freedom, Busher believes that people will come to know the truth through the Spirit and the Word and will be enabled to live uprightly.[30] This has pragmatic appeal to the government by bringing a number of social, economic and political advantages,[31] but Busher's main desire is to see people being gathered to Christ. Persecution only succeeds in giving false assurance or driving them away altogether: "The bishops should understand, that it is preaching, and not persecuting, that getteth people to the church of Christ."[32]

Busher is not the only product of Smyth and Helwys' development of religious liberty, although his work (together with his forebears) should be credited as the foundation for later treatments of the subject.

---

[29] Busher, "Religion's Peace," 49.
[30] Busher, "Religion's Peace," 22–23.
[31] White, "Early Baptist Arguments," 7–8.
[32] Busher, "Religion's Peace," 32.

Newgate Prison

7
John Murton

One last General Baptist that should be noted is John Murton. Murton was part of the original Gainsborough congregation that left England for Holland under Smyth and Helwys' leadership, and was a leader of the London congregation alongside Helwys. When Helwys died, it fell to Murton to lead the congregation.[1] Before this, though, Murton had been a fellow-prisoner of Helwys, incarcerated alongside his pastor in Newgate by 1613.

In 1615, the following anonymous document appeared that may be attributable to Murton: *Objections: answered by way of dialogue wherein is proved by the Law of God: by the law of our land: and by his Maties many testimonies that no man ought to be persecuted for his religion, so he testifie his allegeance by the Oath, appointed by law*.[2] In it, Murton stresses his faithfulness to the king and, as with Busher, allows for the punishment of (actual) traitors and terrorists—an important consideration when addressing someone who, with his parliament, was victim to a failed mass assassination-by-explosion attempt plotted by Roman Catholic would-be revolutionaries.[3] Murton argues that God only accepts worship offered willingly and states: "It is a sure rule in divinitie, that God loves not to plant his church by violence and bloodshed."[4] Later, in 1620, Murton anonymously published the following, with similar aims as the former work: *A most humble supplication of many the Kings Maiesties loyall subiects, ready to testifie all civill obedience, by the oath, as the law of this realme requireth, and that of conscience; who are persecuted, onely for differing in religion, contrary to divine and*

---

[1] Keith E. Durso, *No Armor for the Back: Baptist Prison Writings, 1600s-1700s* (Macon: Mercer, 2007), 34.

[2] Durso, *No Armor for the Back*, 35; James L. Garrett, *Baptist Theology* (Macon: Mercer University Press, 2009), 15; L. Busher, "Religion's Peace: A Plea for Liberty of Conscience," in *Tracts on Liberty of Conscience and Persecution 1614-1661*, ed. Edward B. Underhill (London: J. Haddon, 1846), 28; cf. Slayden A. Yarbrough, "The English Separatist Influence on the Baptist Tradition of Church-State Issues," *Baptist History and Heritage* 20, No. 3 (July, 1985), 22, who attributes it to Helwys.

[3] For more on this, see Antonia Fraser, *The Gunpowder Plot: Terror and Faith in 1605* (London: Weidenfeld and Nicolson, 1996).

[4] Yarbrough, "The English Separatist Influence", 22.

John Murton

*humane testimonies as followeth.*⁵ Murton's message is much the same as his predecessors—he distinguishes between spiritual and civil, promises obedience to all legitimate civil demands, believes religious liberty is good politically and domestically, notes the lack of a New Testament command to persecute, and points to other thriving, more tolerant nations as positive examples of freedom's benefits.⁶ A great part of his significance though, lies in evidence of a link—at least so far as this subject is concerned—between the General and Particular Baptists, at whom we shall now look.

---

⁵ Garrett, *Baptist Theology*, 15; Busher, "Religion's Peace," 28; Durso, *No Armor for the Back*, 35.

⁶ Leon McBeth, *English Baptist Literature on Religious Liberty to 1689* (New York: Arno, 1980), 14–15, 56.

Part Three
Endeavouring to Have a Clear Conscience[1]:
Early Particular Baptists

---

[1] From *"A CONFESSION OF FAITH of seven congregations or churches of Christ in London, which are commonly, but unjustly, called Anabaptists; published for the vindication of the truth and information of the ignorant; likewise for the taking off those aspersions which are frequently, both in pulpit and print, unjustly cast upon them"* (London, 1644), Article LII [*sic*].

A TREATISE
CONCERNING THE LAWFVLL SVBIECT OF *BAPTISME*.

Wherein are handled these Particulars;

The Baptizing of *Infants* confuted; and the Grounds to prove the same answered.

The Covenant God made with *Abraham* and his feed handled, & how the same agrees with the Gentiles & their feed.

The Baptisme administred by an Antichristian Power confuted, as no Ordinance of God, and the Grounds to prove the same answered.

If either Church, or Ordinance be wanting, where they are to be found, and how recovered.

The Covenant and not Baptisme formes the Church, and the manner how.

There is no succession under the New Testament, but what is spiritually by faith in the Word of God.

With some other things examined, and briefly discoursed.

By me *J. S.*

Goe teach all Nations, Baptizing them, Mat. 28. 19.
He that beleeves, and is baptized, shall be saved, Mark. 16. 16.
For by one Spirit are we all baptized into one body, 1 Cor. 12. 13.
Prove all things, and hold fast that which is good, 1 Thes. 5. 21.
Lord God the strength of my salvation, cover thou my head in the day of battell, Psal. 140. 7.

LONDON: Printed in the Yeare, 1643

Book by John Spilsbury, pioneer, Particular Baptist pastor

8
Particular Baptist Origins

The Particular Baptists are so named because they took a more Calvinistic approach to soteriology than did the General Baptists—the "particular" and "general" distinction relates to beliefs about the extent of the atonement. It is important to note that this is not how they identified themselves—in fact, there seems at the time to have been some difficulty in expressing their identity, and therefore identifying.

There are two major approaches to Particular Baptist origins. The first approach, most common in the twentieth-century, proposes that the Particular Baptists were not the result of a division within General Baptist churches, which had grown beyond the initial congregation lead by Helwys and Murton, but developed separately from an independent semi-Separatist church founded in London in 1616 and led by the successive ministries of Henry Jacob, John Lothrop, and Henry Jessey, so sometimes referred to as the Jacob-Lathrop-Jessey or JLJ Church.[1] The second approach views the development of the Particular Baptist churches as more concurrent with that of General Baptists, the outcome of communion and conversation between baptistic believers regardless of soteriological differences, that pre-dates the sharper divide of the mid 1640s and later. An important piece to the puzzle is the question of when and by whom believers' baptism *by immersion* instead of affusion (pouring) was discovered. According to this second view, there is substantial evidence that it was in fact the General Baptists and not the Particular Baptists who first adopted the practice, that they influenced the churches that would become known as "Particular Baptists," and thereby it is not historiographically acceptable to enforce as sharp a divide between the early General and Particular Baptists as has become common.[2] To further complicate things, a more recent proposal strongly critiques this second view and argues for (a very distinct)

---

[1] B. R. White, *The English Baptists of the Seventeenth Century*, A History of the English Baptists 1, 2nd rev. ed. (Didcot, Oxfordshire: The Baptist Historical Society, 1996), Chapter 2; James L. Garrett, *Baptist Theology* (Macon: Mercer University Press, 2009), 51.

[2] Stephen Wright, *The Early English Baptists, 1603-1649* (New York: Boydell Press, 2006).

development out of Calvinistic independent congregationalism, but nonetheless does not agree with the helpfulness of the traditional retrospective taxonomy of "General Baptist" and "Particular Baptist."[3] It is not in the interests of this study to weigh these views. However one chooses to label the seventeenth-century baptistic congregationalists who expressed their beliefs through different Arminian or Calvinistic credobaptist confessions, the fact remains: there were certain fundamental beliefs these people held in common about church identity and practice, which extended to a vision for religious liberty.

It can be reasonably suggested that there was at the very least a greater degree of cross-pollination than some would care to admit. There certainly was a measure of ecclesiological agreement and shared identity, evidenced even later in 1661, when Particular Baptist William Kiffen led pastors of both General and Particular Baptist churches in issuing *The Humble Apology of Some Commonly Called Anabaptists*, to distance themselves from an apocalyptic, radical movement known as "the Fifth Monarchy."[4]

While the chronology of events that led to the first Particular Baptist church may not be entirely clear, without question there was one in London by 1638.[5] The waters may be somewhat muddy as to their primary influences, beyond independent scriptural examination, but whatever view one takes of Particular Baptist origins it cannot be reasonably denied given the evidence available that they dialogued with, and made some reference to, the beliefs and practises of Anabaptist groups and the General Baptists.[6] The branch may be different, but it grew out of the same stump of Non-conformist submission to scriptural authority, in the soil of Separatism, with roots in the sixteenth-century reformation movements, and battered by the violent storms of persecution.

---

[3] Matthew C. Bingham, *Orthodox Radicals: Baptist Identity in the English Revolution* (Oxford: University Press, 2019).

[4] Malcolm B. Yarnell III, "Christopher Blackwood: Exemplar of the Seventeenth-Century Particular Baptists," *Southwestern Journal of Theology* 57, No. 2 (Texas: Southwestern Baptist Theological Seminary, 2015), 193.

[5] Garrett, *Baptist Theology*, 51.

[6] Garrett, *Baptist Theology*, 52; John T. Christian, *Did They Dip? Or, an Examination Into the Act of Baptism as Practiced by the English and American Baptists Before the Year 1641* (Louisville: Baptist Book Concern, 1896), Chapters 5–7; Jennifer Petrik, '"Falsely Called Anabaptists": The Particular Baptist Doctrine of Baptism' (diss., Westminster Seminary California, December 2009), 18; Keith E. Durso, *No Armor for the Back: Baptist Prison Writings, 1600s-1700s* (Macon: Mercer, 2007), 51–52.

Alonzo Chappell, The Landing of Roger Williams in 1636

9
Roger Williams

That there is a link between General Baptist and Particular Baptist views on religious liberty is shown somewhat by the influence John Murton's writings had on Roger Williams. Williams was in the American colonies, not England when he was a Baptist, and he was no longer a Baptist when in 1644 he published his great treatise on religious liberty: *The Bloudy Tenent of Persecution, for Cause of Conscience, Discussed in a Conference between Truth and Peace.* His work might as a result seem out of place in a book focused on early English Baptist contributions to religious liberty. But Williams was an Englishman, he started the first Baptist church in America, his beliefs concerning religious liberty were thoroughly Baptist, and had great influence among Baptists in England—especially the Particular Baptists.[1]

As a Cambridge-educated former Anglican clergyman who sailed from Bristol to Boston, North America in 1630–1631, Williams was described upon his arrival by Governor John Winthrop of Massachusetts Bay Colony as "a Godly minister."[2] William Bradford, one of the *Mayflower* Pilgrims who founded Plymouth Colony in 1620, regarded Williams as "a man godly and zealous, having many precious parts."[3] The very traits these men saw in Williams would ultimately prevent him from participating in their Puritan project, which he saw as corrupt and unjust. Tensions were first observable when Williams rejected the very attractive post of teacher in the church at Boston. He did so because they would not publicly repent of their participation in the Church of England while living there, thereby declaring their separation from it.[4] This was perceived as something of a slight, but the theological - and in the state-church system, political implications were of greater concern. Although

---

[1] Leon McBeth, *English Baptist Literature on Religious Liberty to 1689* (New York: Arno, 1980), 284.

[2] John Winthrop, *Winthrop's Journal: 1630-1649 volume I*, ed. James K. Hosmer (New York: Charles Scribner's Sons, 1908), 1:57.

[3] William Bradford, *Of Plymouth Plantation: 1620-1647* (New York: Modern Library, 1952), 257.

[4] Winthrop, *Journal*, 1:63.

Williams continued to exercise a much-appreciated preaching ministry as a Separatist in both Massachusetts Bay and Plymouth colonies, his beliefs continued to pose a problem for the religious-political establishment of Puritan New England.

In Boston, Williams refused to join the church as its teacher because of his rejection of the state-church system and his objection to the King of England as the head of the church. He also questioned the idea that magistrates had authority—post-Christ's Incarnation—to punish breaches of the first table of the Ten Commandments, as those are matters of individual conscience that cannot be coerced by government but can be compelled by the gospel. After moving to Salem, Williams began to effectively accuse the king and his more loyal subjects not only of wrongly enforcing the first table of the Ten Commandments but breaking second table laws like coveting, theft, and lying. Who was King James I that in 1620 he should give the Massachusetts Bay Company the right to settle lands that had been possessed by Indigenous tribes for thousands of years?[5]

A growing interest in, and sincere concern for, the rights of the Native people around him did not develop separately from Williams' views on church, state, and religious liberty, but out of them. Williams rejected the very concept of "Christendom" and "Christian world," unless referring exclusively to local churches, and so it was absurd to distribute rights to other people's land in the name of a nonexistent Christendom and a blasphemous injustice to exploit others in the name of Christianity.[6] Williams set about pursuing a better way: he began journeying into the New England wilderness, to trade with the Natives, build good relations with them, and to learn their culture and language. By so doing, he could better help them as fellow humans made in God's image, and could tell them the good news about Jesus, waiting on God to open their hearts.[7]

Williams moved to Plymouth and then back to Salem, where he became an elder in the Separatist congregation. He continued to speak strongly against

---

[5] James A. Warren, *God, War, and Providence: the epic struggle of Roger Williams and the Narragansett Indians against the Puritans of New England* (New York: Scribner, 2018), 45.

[6] Cf. Warren, *God, War, and Providence*, 45–50; Glenn W. LaFantasie ed., "The Road to Banishment: Editorial Note," in *The Correspondence of Roger Williams, Vol. I, 1629–1653* (Hanover: Brown University Press, 1988), 14–15.

[7] Cf. Roger Williams, "Christenings make not Christians" in *On Religious Liberty: Selections from the Works of Roger Williams*, ed. James Calvin Davis (Harvard: University Press, 2008), 157–166.

religious coercion and unjust colonisation by the magistrates, which led to his banishment from the Massachusetts Bay Colony, formally on October 9, 1635 and finally in January 1636. In the dead of winter, Williams fled Boston, encouraged by John Winthrop, to a place free of English presence and thus the tyranny of the state-church system: the wilderness lands of his new Native friends, particularly in this instance, the Narragansett tribe.

Williams and others who travelled with him were warmly welcomed by the Narragansetts, who sold them land on which to settle. It was there, in what is now called Rhode Island, that Williams came to Baptist views, was baptised as a believer, and formed America's first Baptist church in 1639 with others baptised on the same occasion.[8] His understanding of man, God, sovereignty, and salvation was Calvinistic, and so he may rightly be referred to at this stage as a Particular Baptist. Fittingly, he called the settlement that he began, "Providence," in honour of the meaningful and meticulous ways in which God had guided and provided. Williams "desired it might be for a shelter for persons distressed of conscience."[9]

Ever unsettled by battles within his conscience and beset by challenges in the turbulent spiritual and civil world around him, Williams ceased to be a Baptist after a very short time. He left the congregation he had begun after only a few months due to a new-found belief that there had to be apostolic succession for baptism to be valid. He was not moving on to another church, since this understanding left him viewing the establishment of visible, local churches as somewhat of a lost cause.[10] He did however retain many Baptist convictions, including the belief in religious liberty for all. Like the early English Baptists before him, Williams was shaped by his exegesis of Scripture and by his experience of persecution, and would become a significant voice in the fight for religious liberty.

---

[8] Erroll Hulse, *An Introduction to the Baptists* (Haywards Heath: Carey Publications, 1976), 51-52; James L. Garrett, *Baptist Theology* (Macon: Mercer University Press, 2009), 110.

[9] From a 1661 deed by Roger Williams, William R. Staples, *Annals of the Town of Providence, from Its First Settlement, to the Organization of the City Government, in June 1832* (Providence: Knowles and Vose, 1843), 30.

[10] Garrett, *Baptist Theology*, 110; Keith E. Durso, *No Armor for the Back: Baptist Prison Writings, 1600s-1700s* (Macon: Mercer, 2007), 198; Roger Williams, "A Biographical Introduction," in *The Bloudy Tenent of Persecution for Cause of Conscience Discussed and Mr. Cotton's Letter Examined and Answered*, ed. Edward Bean Underhill (Kessinger Publishing, 2004), xxvi.

Roger Williams

In 1643, Williams travelled to England to secure a charter for the colony of Providence Plantations.[11] While there, he published *The Bloudy Tenent*. Williams' argument against persecution was that

> It is contrary to certain New Testament texts; the blood of many martyrs has been shed; civil magistrates ought not to govern Christian faith and worship; there is a marked difference between a literal sword and the sword of the Spirit (the Word of God); and religious uniformity is provocative of civil wars, discourages the conversion of Jews to Christ, and confuses the civil and the religious.[12]

Arguing from Scripture, Williams finds no evidence that civil authorities should use the sword to promote or persecute religion of any kind in Romans 13:1–7. Quite the opposite is demonstrated in his interpretation of the parable of the tares. In a stronger though somewhat similar statement to that made by Helwys, Williams says that:

> It is the will and command of God, that (since the comming of his Sonne the Lord Jesus) a permission of the most Paganish, Jewish, Turkish, or Anti-Christian consciences and worships bee granted to all men in all Nations and Countries: and they are only to bee fought against with that Sword which is only (in Soule matters), able to conquer, to wit, the Sword of God's Spirit, the Word of God.[13]

He draws on Murton's work at some length and is clearly inspired by this—to him anonymous—"close prisoner to Newgate," relating how apparently Murton had no use of pen and ink and so wrote with milk on paper meant as a stopper for his milk bottle, sending the invisible manuscript home with a friend to be transcribed in front of a fire.[14] Whether the story is true or apocryphal we cannot say but it, together with Murton's writings themselves, had an impact on Williams.[15]

---

[11] Durso, *No Armor for the Back*, 198.

[12] Garrett, *Baptist Theology*, 112; cf. Ian M. Randall, *Communities of Conviction: Baptist Beginnings in Europe* (Schwarzenfeld: Neufeld Verlag, 2009), 15, taken from William's introductory summary.

[13] Roger Williams, *The Bloudy Tenent of Persecution for Cause of Conscience*, ed. S. L. Caldwell (R.I.: Providence, The Narragansett Club, 1867), 3.

[14] Williams, *The Bloudy Tenent*, 61.

[15] John Coffey, "Puritanism and Liberty Revisited: The Case for Toleration in the English Revolution," *Historical Journal* 41, No. 4 (December, 1998): 965; Durso, *No Armor for the Back*,

In summary, Williams believed that salvation for a sinful, lost, and broken humanity is found only in Jesus Christ as people trust in him, that authentic faith in Christ cannot and should not be coerced, that the Scriptures are sufficient, that the gospel—not government—is God's power for salvation, and the pleadings of the Holy Spirit—not pressure from a hypocritical state—is what will draw people into Christ's Kingdom. Interpreting the parable of the tares, or briars, Williams wrote with hope: "He that is a *Briar*, that is, a *Jew*, a *Turke*, a *Pagan*, [or] an *Antichristian* today, may be (when the Word of the *Lord* runs freely), a member of Jesus Christ tomorrow."[16]

The Bloudy Tenent was not well received by most professedly Christian groups in England. Presbyterianism was on the rise, and its adherents in particular "exclaimed against it as full of heresy and blasphemy." By order of parliament, copies of the book were seized and burned in the streets.[17] Even Independents, with whom Baptists might have enjoyed more affinity, were uncomfortable with the broad vision of liberty Williams proposed, and could only extend it to those sound in the fundamentals of the Christian faith.[18] And yet, that vision continued to be embraced by the Baptists, who were continuing their peaceful fight for freedom. In Rhode Island and Providence Plantations, it continued to be carried forward by Baptist believers. One of these was John Clarke, co-founder with Williams of the colony, and founder of America's second Baptist church, in Newport. Surrounded by hostile colonies, the Suffolk-born Clarke fought for and achieved something systemically seismic: the Rhode Island Royal Charter of 1663, which is notable not only for acknowledging Indigenous people's rights to the land and forming a democratic republic within the colony, but also for securing—for the first time in history—a monarch's guarantee to peaceful religious practice without any government interference.[19]

36; Thomas White, "'The Defense of Religious Liberty' by the Anabaptists and the English Baptists," in *First Freedom: The Baptist Perspective on Religious Liberty*, eds. Thomas White, Jason B. Duesing, and Malcolm B. Yarnell III (Nashville: B&H, 2007), 64.

[16] Williams, *The Bloudy Tenent*, 95.

[17] Underhill, "A Biographical Introduction," xxxiv.

[18] Underhill, "A Biographical Introduction", xxxv.

[19] Cf. Samuel Greene Arnold, *History of the State of Rhode Island and Providence Plantations: 1636-1700, Vol. 1* (New York: Appleton and Broadway, 1859), 290-295; Warren, *God, War, and Providence*, 187.

A CONFESSION OF FAITH

Of seven Congregations or Churches of Christ in LONDON, which are commonly (but uniustly) called Anabaptists.

PUBLISHED

For the vindication of the Truth, and information of the ignorant; likewise for the taking off of those aspersions which are frequently both in Pulpit and Print unjustly cast upon them.

But this I confesse unto thee, that after the way which they call heresie, so worship I the God of my Fathers, beleeving all things that are written in the Law and the Prophets, and have hope towards God, which they themselves also allow, that there shall be a resurrection of dead both of the just and unjust. Acts 24. 14, 15.
For we cannot but speak the things that we have seen and heard, Acts 4.20.
If I have spoken evill, beare witnesse of the evill; but if well, why smitest thou me? John 18. 23.
Blessed are yee when men revile you, and say all manner of evill against you falsly for my sake. Rejoyce, &c. Matth. 5.11.12. & 19.29.

The second Impression corrected and enlarged.

Published according to Order.

London printed by *Matth. Simmons*, and are to be sold by *John Hancock* in Popes-head Alley. 1 6 4 6.

First London Baptist Confession of Faith 1644 (revised 1646)

10
The First London Baptist Confession

After a period of relative quiet in which their voices were suppressed, Baptist believers, especially those from the newly formed Particular Baptist churches, emerged with a vigour that was quite intolerable to their adversaries. Their pleas for religious liberty were especially noisome to the Presbyterian Thomas Edwards who wrote with disgust:

> there have been more Books writ, Sermons preached, words spoken, besides plottings and actings for a Toleration, within these foure last years, then for all other things. Every day now brings forth Books for a Toleration.[1]

The same year as Williams' *Bloudy Tenent* was published, the first edition of a confession of faith was drawn up by the seven Particular Baptist churches in London, and was later revised in 1646. This first London Baptist Confession makes several statements, with scriptural proofs, that provide a theological framework for religious liberty. Article 33 emphasises the *spiritual* nature of Christ's Kingdom on Earth, Article 34 designates the church (not the nation) as the recipient of Christ's promises and covenant, Article 36 gives the power to choose church officers to the members of the church alone (not heads of state), Articles 39 and 40 uphold the baptism of believers only by immersion, and the membership of a local church (not some external party) is responsible for church discipline according to Articles 42–44. These articles undercut the thinking of the Erastian system enforced in those days.

With Article 48, the subject of the civil magistrate begins to be addressed: government is set up by God for punishing evil and praising good, there should be submission to all lawful commands, and Christians should lift up government leaders in prayer. Any ecclesiastical laws that go against conscience,

---

[1] Leon McBeth, *English Baptist Literature on Religious Liberty to 1689* (New York: Arno, 1980), 14–15, 70.

however, they cannot rightly submit to (Art. 49) and so would bless God if the magistrates were inclined

> to tender our consciences, as that we might be protected by them from wrong, injury, oppression and molestation, which long we formerly have groaned under by the tyranny and oppression of the Prelatical Hierarchy...[2]

The remaining points express that these Baptists will submit as appropriate to God and government, but will not disobey God in order to please or placate man. In conclusion they make their resolve very clear:

> But if any man shall impose upon us anything that we see not to be commanded by our Lord Jesus Christ, we should in His strength, rather embrace all reproaches and tortures of men, to be stript of all outward comforts, and if it were possible, to die a thousand deaths, rather than to do anything against the least tittle of the truth of God, or against the light of our own consciences.[3]

Distancing themselves from claims associating them with the more isolationist tendencies of some Anabaptists, the 1646 revision of the Confession says that "it is lawful for a Christian to be a magistrate or civil officer."[4] Their problem was not with governmental offices, nor with Christians holding such offices. Rather they were concerned with the proper and biblical use of those offices. To intrude in matters of religion is, after Christ and the institution of the new covenant, beyond the bounds of government.

---

[2] *"A Confession of Faith of seven congregations or churches of Christ in London, which are commonly, but unjustly, called Anabaptists; published for the vindication of the truth and information of the ignorant; likewise for the taking off those aspersions which are frequently, both in pulpit and print, unjustly cast upon them"* (London, 1644), Article L.

[3] *A Confession of Faith* (1644), Conclusion.

[4] From *"A Confession of Faith of seven congregations or churches of Christ in London, which are commonly, but unjustly, called Anabaptists..."* 2nd ed. (London, 1646).

11
Samuel Richardson

The Confession's fifteen signatories were well aware that religious liberty was the logical consequence of their document's theological content. John Spilsbury, often identified as the first Particular Baptist pastor, wrote unequivocally in the year before the 1644 Confession, "no conscience ought to be forced in the matters of Religion, because no man can beare out another in his account to God, if in case he should cause him to sinne."[1] Another of the signatories was layman Samuel Richardson: a man about whom little is known other than he had influence, access, and was an active proponent of full toleration in religious matters.[2] When civil war broke out between the King and parliament and their respective supporters, Richardson supported the Parliamentarians, as they would grant a greater measure of religious liberty than Charles I and his Royalist allies.[3]

In 1647, Richardson published a tract entitled *The Necessity of Toleration in all Matters of Religion*. He grounds his argument in the will of God and the nature of true worship and worshippers:

> it is God's way to have Religion free, and only to flow from an inward principle of faith and love; neither would God be worshipped by unwilling worshippers.[4]

Really then, there can be no such thing as compelling people to "true worship," as it is voluntary.[5]

---

[1] "*John Spilsbury's personal confession of ten articles for the Godly reader to judge, what difference there is between him and me, in the main, that men should be so incensed against me, as to seek my life, as some have done*" (London, 1643), Article No. 8.

[2] John Coffey, "Puritanism and Liberty Revisited: The Case for Toleration in the English Revolution," *Historical Journal*, 41, No. 4 (December, 1998): 967.

[3] Jennifer R. Stoddard, "Seventeenth Century Particular Baptist Views on Religious Liberty" (MA thesis, Westminster Seminary, California, 2011), 67.

[4] Samuel Richardson, *The Necessity of Toleration in Matters of Religion* ... (London, 1647), 4.

[5] Leon McBeth, *English Baptist Literature on Religious Liberty to 1689* (New York: Arno, 1980), 106.

The centrepiece of Richardson's work is a series of seventy questions, which the longer version of the title explains are intended *to prove that Corporeal Punishment ought not to be inflicted upon such as hold Errors in Religion, and that in matters of Religion, men ought not to be compelled, but have liberty and freedom.*[6] The first question he asks is "Whether corporal punishment can open blind eyes, and give light to dark understandings?"[7] Other questions include: "Whether carnall punishments can produce any more then a carnall repentance and obedience," "Whether the Saints weapons against errors, be carnall or no" (citing 2 Cor. 10:4), "Whether Christ hath said, He will have an unwilling people compelled to serve him," and "Whether ever God did plant his church by violence and bloud-shed?"[8] Also included in his seventy questions are pastoral concerns such as the possibility of "eleventh-hour" conversions, the proper exercise of church discipline, and the Christian response to persecution, as well as practical concerns such as the reality of fallible judges.[9]

The dangers of a state-enforced religion are apparent to Richardson from a number of angles. What would the impact be on families, should one partner—say, the husband, be a heretic but his wife and children are not? What if the state-enforced religion hardens people against the Christian faith by tyrannically forcing it upon them? What if the state-enforced religion leads to *en masse* apostasy away from the biblical gospel? What if the only religion permitted is that approved by the government, and the government approves of no religion, resulting in a constitutionally atheist state? How should churches approach congregational gatherings when the state tells them not to and should they be dependent on the consent of Magistrates or the commands of God and apostolic practice? Of course there is also the matter of hypocrisy: how can Protestants be angry with totalitarian, tyrannical regimes that persecute people who are considered to be in error or heretical, if their own approach would be little different?[10]

---

[6] The full title of the book acts as a table of contents: *The Necessity of Toleration in all Matters of Religion; or, certain questions propounded to the Synod, tending to prove that Corporeal Punishment ought not to be inflicted upon such as hold Errors in Religion, and that in matters of Religion, men ought not to be compelled, but have liberty and freedom. Here is also copy of the Edict of the Emperors Constantinus and Licinius, and containing the Reasons that enforced them to grant unto all men liberty to choose and follow what Religion they thought best. Also, here is the faith of the Assembly of Divines, as it was taken out of the exactest copy of their practice, with the Nonconformists' Answer why they cannot receive and submit to the said faith.*

[7] Richardson, *The Necessity of Toleration*, 5.
[8] Richardson, *The Necessity of Toleration*, 5–7.
[9] Richardson, *The Necessity of Toleration*, 5–7.
[10] Richardson, *The Necessity of Toleration*, 9–10.

Every Man's Conscience

Richardson's belief in religious liberty for all did not prevent him from calling out against the perceived errors of religious groups in his day. Rather it necessitated it – the nation's spiritual vitality was at stake! The *frontis* of the book effectively equates the Anglican Church of the day with Rome and lays the blame for the dearth of spiritual light and life in the land squarely at its feet:

> "Where Romish Tyrannie hath the upper hand,
> Darkness of minde, and superstition stand."[11]

He was equally wary of Presbyterianism's claims to offer a suitable alternative, saying of the Westminster Divines, "we had as good be under the Pope as under your Presbyterian check."[12] The poet John Milton famously expressed along the same lines that "New Presbyter is but Old Priest writ Large," in his poem, *On the new forcers of Conscience under Long Parliament*.[13] Neither the state having authority over religious faith and practice, nor the majority religion having authority over the state would end well. Permitting religious liberty so that individuals might freely proclaim, debate, discuss, and hopefully come to faith in Christ was, for Richardson, what would bring authentic spiritual regeneration and social renewal, not setting up another system of compulsion.

---

[11] Richardson, *The Necessity of Toleration*, frontis.
[12] Stoddard, "Seventeenth Century Particular Baptist Views," 67.
[13] John Milton, *On the New Forcers of Conscience under the Long Parliament* (London, 1646).

*Thomas Venner, Fifth Monarchy leader,
woodcut by unknown artist, late eighteenth century*

12
Particular Baptist Religious Liberty— for Everyone?

Were Particular Baptists in favour of religious liberty for *everyone*? It would be inaccurate to make such a statement covering all English Baptists without exception, although those with a narrower approach to liberty are most certainly out of step with the majority of Baptists (General and Particular) and not at all representative of the whole. The overwhelming and consistent Baptist approach was of complete religious liberty for all, whatever their religion or lack of religion.[1] Any exceptions simply prove the rule.

The most liberty that Baptists had hitherto enjoyed came during the Protectorate of Oliver Cromwell. After decades of persecution, marginalisation, and state interference with religious life, Baptists and other religious Non-conformists enjoyed a measure of peace and even attained a certain degree of power that was unthinkable under previous monarchs. For the first time in English history, the head of state could be heard saying things like:

> Again, is not Liberty of Conscience in Religion a Fundamental? So long as there is Liberty of Conscience for the Supreme Magistrate to exercise his conscience in erecting what Form of Church-Government he is satisfied he should set up ... why should he not give the like liberty to others? Liberty of Conscience is a natural right; and he that would have it, ought to give it; having 'himself' liberty to settle what he likes for the Public ... All the money of this Nation would not have tempted men to fight upon such an account as they have here been engaged in, if they had not had hopes of Liberty "of Conscience" better than Episcopacy granted them, or than would have been afforded by a Scots Presbytery,—or an English either.[2]

---

[1] Leon McBeth, *English Baptist Literature on Religious Liberty to 1689* (New York: Arno, 1980), 276-277.

[2] Oliver Cromwell, "SPEECH III," First Parliament, 12 September 1656, in *Oliver Cromwell's Letters and Speeches, Vol. 2*, ed. Thomas Carlyle (New York: Harper and Brothers, 1868), 121.

Religious Liberty for Everyone?

A new era seemed to dawn, and one which seemed to be moving in the direction of religious liberty as Baptists had envisioned it. Roger Williams heard Cromwell speak at a committee level, and reported:

> at a Debate of the Honourable Committee, and in a confluence of many Auditors; when it pleased an Honourable Gentleman of the Committee, zealously to argue against a Laodicean, and lukewarm indifferency in Religion, professing for his part, That he had rather be a Saul than a Gallio. His Excellency with much Christian zeal and affection for his own Conscience professed also, That he had rather that Mahumetanism were permitted amongst us, than that one of Gods Children should be persecuted.[3]

This kind of language, along with good diplomatic relations with the Ottoman Empire and the publication of an English translation of the Quran (initially seized but eventually permitted by the new government), had establishmentarian zealots accusing Cromwell of being a new "Mahomet."[4]

In light of the favourable regime change, an English Particular Baptist couple petitioned the government from their home in Amsterdam to reverse the national ban on Jews in England. They wrote as Christians "conversant ... with and amongst some of Izraells race, called Jewes, and growing sensible of their heavy out-cryes and clamours against the intolerable cruelty of this our English Nation" who desired that their Jewish neighbours "come to know the Emanuell, the Lord of life, light, and glory; even as we are known of him" and also wanted to assist in the reparative justice of restoring the global Jewish diaspora to their Middle Eastern homeland from which they had been displaced. It was time "that the inhumane cruel Statute of banishment made against them, may be repealed, and they under the Christian baner of charity, and brotherly love, may again be received and permitted to dwell amongst you in this Land, as now they do in the Nether-lands."[5]

Pleas of this nature continued, led especially by the Jewish scholar Rabbi Mennaseh Ben Israel (also based in Amsterdam). Cromwell convened the

---

[3] Roger Williams, "To the truly Christian reader," in *The fourth paper, presented by Major Butler, to the Honourable Committee of Parliament, for the propagating the gospel of Christ Jesus* (1651).

[4] John V. Tolan, *Faces of Muhammad: Western Perceptions of the Prophet of Islam from the Middle Ages to Today* (Princeton: Princeton University Press, 2019), 12, 72, 140.

[5] *The Petition of the Jewes for the Repealing of the Act of Parliament for their banishment out of England. Presented to his Excellency and the generall Councell of Officers on Fryday Jan. 5. 1648* (London, 1648).

Whitehall Conference in 1655 to discuss Jewish readmission, but sensing those gathered were of a less tolerant disposition, brought proceedings to halt. Even if the nation's front door could not be opened without uproar, Cromwell hoped the back door might still open. It did in 1656 and 1657, when the secret Jewish presence in London was implicitly acknowledged, and Jews were permitted to worship, to open a synagogue, and to lease a cemetery.

Though still far away from the true realisation of the Baptist vision for religious liberty, the winds were blowing favourably in the right direction. There were however individuals here and there who fell short of embracing the totality of this Baptist distinctive, while still claiming Baptist identity. Some Baptists could be found among the revolutionary Fifth Monarchists, for example. The Fifth Monarchy was a mid-seventeenth-century interdenominational movement that included non-violent and violent participants who interpreted biblical prophecies - especially those of Daniel 2—through the lens of current events, and believed that they would see Christ's 1000 year reign from Revelation 20 established in their lifetime.[6] Of course, the interpretive method was all very Anglo-centric, oriented around political developments in the British Isles, without much consideration to the global scene or to more sober-minded exegesis of the biblical texts.[7]

The defeat of the Royalists and consequent execution of King Charles I in 1649 was regarded as the end of the Daniel prophecy's fourth kingdom. However, the beginning of the short-lived Protectorate system under Oliver Cromwell in 1651 did not lead to Christ's millennial Kingdom, and the years after Cromwell's death in 1658 were so chaotic that even old opponents of the king moved to restore the monarchy under Charles II. The tipping point for this development was Charles' *Declaration of Breda* in 1660, which includes a seemingly strong statement for religious liberty, that acknowledges differences in society and encourages intelligent dialogue:

---

[6] Anthony L. Chute, Nathan A. Finn, and Michael A. G. Haykin eds., *The Baptist Story: From English Sect to Global Movement* (Nashville: B&H Publishing, 2015), 40–42; For a more detailed study see Bernard Capp, *The Fifth Monarchy Men: A Study in Seventeenth Century Millenarianism* (London: Faber and Faber, 2011).

[7] This approach to reading the news of current events into the Scriptures (distinct from deriving encouragement from the Scriptures to face current events) was not uncommon. See Crawford Gribben, "Baptists and Millennialism in Early Modern England", in *Exploring Baptist Origins*, eds. Anthony R. Cross and Nicholas J. Wood (Oxford: Centre for Baptist History and Heritage, Regents Park College, 2010), 101-121.

And because the passion and uncharitablnesse of the times have produced several opinions in Religion, by which men are engaged in parties and animosities against each other, which when they shall hereafter unite in a freedom of conversation will be composed or better understood: We do declare a Liberty to Tender Consciences, and that no man shall be disquieted or called in question for differences of opinion in matters of Religion, which do not disturb the Peace of the Kingdom.[8]

Very much the opposite proved to be the case during the Restoration period, which attempted to turn back the clock on any toleration or liberty enjoyed by religious Non-conformists. Not even those within the established Church of England escaped: failure to conform to the 1660 Act for Confirming and Restoring of Ministers and the 1662 Act of Uniformity led to thousands being ejected from ministerial positions, replaced by High Church Loyalists to the king.[9]

The 1662 Act of Uniformity was one of four acts passed from 1661–1665 collectively called the Clarendon Code. The 1661 Corporation Act stated that no one could enter elected office if they had not first "taken the Sacrament of the Lords Supper according to the Rites of the Church of England" within the past year.[10] The 1662 Act of Uniformity compelled the use of the Book of Common Prayer in worship, and required that a minister "openly and publiquely before the Congregation there assembled declare his unfeigned assent & consent to the use of all things in the said Booke contained and prescribed."[11] The 1664 Conventicle Act criminalised anyone over the age of sixteen gathering with more than five from different households for an "Assembly Conventicle or Meeting under colour or pretence of any Exercise of Religion in other manner then is allowed by the Liturgy or practise of the Church of England."[12] Finally, the Five Mile Act in 1665 forbade those ministers who were expelled

---

[8] King Charles II, *His declaration to all his loving subjects of the kingdom of England. Dated from his Court at Breda in Holland, the 4/14 of April 1660. And read in Parliament, May, 1. 1660. Together with his Majesties letter of the same date, to his Excellence the Lord General Monck, to be communicated to the Lord President of the Council of State, and to the officers of the army under his command* (Edinburgh; reprint, by Christopher Higgins, in Harts Close, over against the Trone-Church, 1660).

[9] For an introduction to this event, see Gary Brady, *The Great Ejection 1662: Today's Evangelicalism Rooted in Puritan Persecution* (Darlington: Evangelical Press, 2012).

[10] John Raithby ed., "Charles II, 1661: An Act for the Well Governing and Regulating of Corporations," in *Statutes of the Realm: Vol. 5, 1628-80* (n.p., 1819), 321-323.

[11] John Raithby, *Statutes of the Realm*, 364-370.

[12] John Raithby, *Statutes of the Realm*, 516-520.

for not swearing total allegiance to the king and using the government approved liturgy from living within five miles of the city or town from which they were expelled.[13]

Not even London's relatively new coffee houses escaped Charles II's insecure gaze. Despite the economic benefits they brought to the Crown in coffee excise taxes, coffee houses were viewed as a threat to the developing new order. This was not unfounded: they were centres for news circulation, literature distribution, discussion, and debate, frequented by Dissenters. At least one London Baptist pastor at the time, James Jones, is known to have run a coffee house, and coffee houses were the launch pad for Baptist church planting, associations, and pastors' fraternals.[14] They too became targets of government policing and oppressive legislation. On December 29, 1675, King Charles II proclaimed the following:

> Whereas it is most apparent, that the Multitude of Coffee-Houses of late years set up and kept within this Kingdom, the Dominion of Wales, and the Town of Berwick upon Tweed, and the great resort of idle and disaffected persons to them, have produced very evil and dangerous effects; as well for that many Tradesmen and others, do therein misspend much of their time, which might and probably would otherwise be employed in and about their Lawful Callings and Affairs; but also, for that in such Houses, and by occasion of the meetings of such persons therein, divers false, malitious and scandalous reports are devised and spread abroad, to the Defamation of His Majesties Government, and to the disturbance of the Peace and Quiet of the Realm; His Majesty hath thought it fit and necessary, that the said Coffee-houses be (for the future) put down and suppressed, and doth (with the advice of His Privy Council) by this His Royal Proclamation, Strictly Charge and Command all manner of persons, that they or any of them do not presume from and after the Tenth Day of January next ensuing, to keep any Publick Coffee-house, or to utter or sell by retail, in his, her or their house or houses (to be spent or consumed within the same) any Coffee,

---

[13] John Raithby, *Statutes of the Realm*, 575.

[14] Baptist Union Publication Department, "Notes and Query," in *Transactions of the Baptist Historical Society*, 3, No. 3 (May, 1913): 191; Isaac Marlow, "James Jones's Coffee-House," *The Baptist Quarterly* 6, No. 7 (July, 1933): 324–326; William Thomas Whitley, *A Baptist Bibliography, Vol. I* (Hildesheim: Georg Olms, 1984), 221; Michael A.G. Haykin, *The Weekly Historian: 52 Reflections on Church History* (Peterborough: H&E, 2021), 119.

Religious Liberty for Everyone?

Chocolet, Sherbett or Tea, as they will answer the contrary at their utmost perils.[15]

This proved completely unenforceable and unsuccessful, but demonstrates the fragility of the restored monarchy and with it, the return of the elitist High Church establishment.

Revolutionary impulses thrived in the soil of persecution, nostalgia, and hope. The end-times obsession of the Fifth Monarchy movement led some down the path of violent insurrection. For them, Cromwell's Protectorate may actually have hindered the establishment of Christ's reign, and the Restoration of the monarchy certainly did. The Kingdom would have to be established by force. Charles II scarcely had an opportunity to begin his more oppressive agenda when a group of Fifth Monarchy men staged an insurrection on January 6, 1661. Led by Thomas Venner, who had similarly plotted an uprising against Cromwell, they stormed St. Paul's Cathedral, and proclaimed Christ as King. The revolt was put down after a few days, with loss of life on both sides, followed by the inevitable trials and executions: Venner himself was hung, drawn, and quartered.[16]

Baptists had no problem affirming Christ as King, nor were they averse to civil disobedience or even resistance if appropriate and necessary. But they were opposed to confusing Christ's Kingdom with those of this world, and the accompanying fantasy that Christ's Kingdom could be ushered in by an armed revolution of the people, any more than it could be established by legislative or violent coercion from the state. Because of their commitment to nonconformity, however, the accusation of Fifth Monarchy sympathies became the new reason for investigating, apprehending, and incarcerating Baptist believers. Any Baptists who may have held common cause with revolutionary Fifth Monarchists were, however, disowned from any connection at all with the Baptists—keen to note that only one of the Venner rebels did not assert infant baptism. Thirty signatories including Particular Baptist William Kiffen and General Baptist Thomas Lambe wrote in *The Humble Apology of Some Commonly Called Anabaptists*: "the persons not being of our belief or practice about

---

[15] King Charles II, *A Proclamation for the Suppression of Coffee-Houses* (London, John Bill and Christopher Barker, 1675); for more on this, cf. Brian Cowan, *The Social Life of Coffee: The Emergence of the British Coffeehouse* (New Haven: Yale, 2005).

[16] Champlin Burrage, "The Fifth Monarchy Insurrections," in *The English Historical Review*, Vol. 25, Issue C, ed. Reginald L. Poole (London: Longmans, Greene And Co., 1910), 722-747.

Baptism, but, to the best of our information, they were all (except one) assertors of Infant Baptism, and never had communion with us in our assemblies."[17]

In short, the politics of Christ's Kingdom by state coercion or people's revolution were the preserve of a paedobaptist ecclesiology, not a Baptist one. Though some individuals caught up in various political movements for one reason or another may have been "Baptists," their beliefs and behaviour with regard to the Kingdom, and how to treat people of other beliefs, were not distinctively Baptist. In general, Baptists have been at the forefront of the struggle for true freedom of religion.[18]

It has nevertheless been argued that there were fundamental differences between the General and Particular Baptists on the subject of religious liberty, and the claim is made that the Particular Baptists took a moderate position between Roman Catholicism, Anglicanism, and Presbyterianism on the one hand, and the General Baptists on the other.[19] This not only goes against scholarly consensus, but misrepresents the General Baptist position to appear so broad as to be naïve and without any caveats (such as national security). It is possible that such an approach is a matter of using a biased historiographic method that views everything through the lens of contemporary Calvinist-Arminian controversies—neglecting the historic cooperation of Particular and General Baptists (as seen in *The Humble Apology*), particularly in light of a hostile culture. But this misconception might also very well be due to a misreading or incomplete reading of relevant texts. One of the Particular Baptists sometimes cited, even by those who do not hold this view in its entirety, is Christopher Blackwood, who apparently is a primary example of a Baptist who was not for *universal* liberty in religious matters. If indeed he presents us with a potential deviation from the norm, or provides us with the key to unlock an alternative understanding of the Particular Baptist concept of religious liberty, it is important to now investigate him and his writings.

---

[17] William Kiffen et al., *The humble apology of some commonly called Anabaptists, in behalf of themselves and others of the same judgement...* (London, 1661), 17.

[18] Malcolm B. Yarnell III, "The Development of Religious Liberty: A Survey of its Progress and Challenges in Christian History," *Journal for Baptist Theology and Ministry*, 6, No. 1 (spring, 2009): 125.

[19] Jennifer R. Stoddard, "Seventeenth Century Particular Baptist Views on Religious Liberty" (MA thesis, Westminster Seminary, California, 2011), 48.

Seventeenth-Century Map of Ireland

13
Christopher Blackwood

Christopher Blackwood served as an Anglican rector and curate in south-east England during the early 1630s, although there is some evidence that he had Non-conformist sympathies.[1] It seems that at some point he went to New England, possibly as a result of religious persecution, but returned to Kent in 1642, where in 1644 he heard a discourse delivered by a General Baptist named Francis Cornwell. The message prompted Blackwood to investigate Cornwell's claims that infant baptism was without biblical justification and went against Christ and his people. A time was set for him to report his findings to fellow sceptics and when he did it was "not a refutation of Mr. Cornwell's sentiments, but a confirmation of them" that he brought.[2] Blackwood became a Baptist—though not a General Baptist since he believed in particular redemption.[3] He eventually went with the Parliamentary army to Ireland, where he planted a church at Wexford, before moving to Kilkenny, subsequently becoming overseer of a church in Dublin, and would be particularly influential among Baptists in Ireland.[4]

In 1644, shortly after his entry into Baptist life, Blackwood published *Storming of Antichrist in his two last and strongest Garrisons, of Compulsion of Conscience and Infants Baptisme.* The *frontis* of Blackwood's work indicates that it is written against cruelty, inequality, and injustice of compulsion of conscience "out of his earnest desire he hath to a thorow Reformation, having

---

[1] Douglas Brown, "Christopher Blackwood: Portrait of a Seventeenth Century Baptist," *The Baptist Quarterly* 32, No. 1 (January, 1987): 28.

[2] A. Taylor, *The English General Baptists of the Seventeenth Century* (London, 1815), 110; Blackwood's story is yet another link between General and Particular Baptists.

[3] Taylor, *The English General Baptists*, 110; Brown, "Christopher Blackwood," 30.

[4] Christopher Blackwood, *Exposition of Matthew Chapters One to Ten* (London, 1659), "To the Reader"; Mark R. Bell, *Apocalypse How?: Baptist Movements during the English Revolution* (Macon: Mercer, 2000), 149; For more on Blackwood and his significance, see Yarnell, "Christopher Blackwood," 181-205 and Paul L. Panter, "Reclaiming Christopher Blackwood for Baptist Historiography: A Pioneer for Particular Baptists and the Oracle of the English Baptists to Ireland 1605-1670" (D.Phil. diss., Midwestern Baptist Theological Seminary, May 2022).

formerly seen the mischeifs of half Reformations."⁵ First of all, his desire is for purity of worship. He believes this can be accomplished when an assembly is seen to be comprised of officers, members, those who are being discipled, and mere hearers, the first two of these alone being "the church." This of course does nothing to build a national church, which Blackwood calls "a foolish dream," but ultimately it leads to liberty of conscience, "That we behaving ourselves peaceably in the common-wealth, and yeelding due obedience to the Civill Magistrate … may have liberty to worship the Lord according to that light revealed unto us."⁶

Blackwood asks "Whether it is lawfull for any person whatsoever to compel the conscience?" In no way does he take the edge off his answer: "It is not."⁷ How then might he be used to demonstrate that Particular Baptists placed more limits on liberty than their General counterparts?

There are astonishing levels of apparent self-contradiction in *Storming of Antichrist*. In the main body of the first part of the work, Blackwood expounds twenty-nine points against compulsion of conscience in matters of religion. Many of these appear explicitly to advocate the same universal liberty advocated by other early Baptists. For example

> To force Papists and prophane multitudes, whether they will or no, to joyne in one worship, one word, Baptisme, Supper and Identity of communion, is not according to the word; but though it carrie the specious show of a glorious uniformity, yet doth it beget nothing but a politick hypocriticall faith, which changes according to the vicissitude of Armies in time of warre, and the multitude of Princes, States, and humane Lawes, in time of Peace.⁸

He argues that we are to win people to the truth only through the sword of the Spirit, which is the word of God, and not through carnal weapons and persecution. Another two of his points relate to being a winsome testimony to Jews, Muslims, and the heathen people-groups of the world, who will come to faith "out of the strength they see in the truth, not by compulsion of fines,

---

⁵ Christopher Blackwood, *Storming of Antichrist in his two last and strongest Garrisons, of Compulsion of Conscience and Infants Baptisme…* (London, 1644), frontis.
⁶ Blackwood, *Storming of Antichrist*, 11.
⁷ Blackwood, *Storming of Antichrist*, 13.
⁸ Blackwood, *Storming of Antichrist*, 16.

banishment, imprisonment, &c."⁹ If persecution of unbelieving people continues, they will be hardened against Christianity, and where they have power, may deny Christians' freedom.¹⁰ Also, so long as Protestants permit and promote the persecution of Catholics, Catholics will do the same to Protestants. He says that "I have heard it related that when sundry Protestants in France complained against persecution, the Papists made this answer; that we doe no otherwise than your own Doctor Calvin allowes."¹¹

However, in a segment where Blackwood is discussing various objections to his argument, he makes statements that appear to go completely against everything he has argued beforehand. One objection is: "Magistrates are to be a terror to evil workers, Rom. 13. But heresie is an evil work."¹² Blackwood answers by noting three types of evil: works against the light of nature and reason, against the light of the nations, and against the light of faith. The first two categories contain evils he considers punishable by the civil authorities, whereas the last category does not.

Works against the light of nature and reason include idolatry (he singles out Islam, polytheistic religion, and atheism) and blasphemy in addition to other offences that may be summarised as crimes against person, property, and princes.¹³ It would seem from this that Muslims and other unbelievers are supposed to be persecuted after all!

Works against the light of the nations are set in the context of a nation with a Christian majority. In such a situation the Magistrate, Blackwood says, may punish any who rail against Christ, deny the Scriptures to be his word, and claim that the epistles were only profitable for the particular churches to whom they were originally written. What is his rationale? To quote him directly: "Because all or most Nations in the world do it."¹⁴ That sort of argumentation is not good enough for him elsewhere, so it is curious that he employs it at this point.

As if he couldn't seem more inconsistent, Blackwood explores the area of evils committed against the light of faith: denial of Christ, participating in false worship, unbelief, impenitence, heresy, and schism. It appears that Blackwood does another about face, and says of these "the Magistrate cannot be a terror

---

[9] Blackwood, *Storming of Antichrist*, 21.
[10] Blackwood, *Storming of Antichrist*, 21.
[11] Blackwood, *Storming of Antichrist*, 16.
[12] Blackwood, *Storming of Antichrist*, 23.
[13] Blackwood, *Storming of Antichrist*, 23.
[14] Blackwood, *Storming of Antichrist*, 23.

unto."[15] In the pages that follow he warns that violence will exasperate people but not win them, separates civil and spiritual into different spheres of authority, and is quite clear that: "We have no command to root out any for conscience, and lesse then a command will not serve, nor have wee any example in the New Testament for the same."[16]

Is Blackwood simply vacillating? We must not forget that he was not long a Baptist when he published these views. He was still reforming his theology and *Storming of the Antichrist* is evidence of his real struggle to do so.[17] It is not his only work, though, and we are mistaken if we read it in isolation. It seems that critics picked up on his flaws and Blackwood wrote a response, entitled *Apostolicall Baptisme*. He returns to the three types of evil named in his former work and admits to having second thoughts about some of what he had said, making the following statement:

> But though my soule abhorre all such opinions, as I do hell, yet do I doubt, whether the Magistrate have any power to deale with any such offender, unlesse he or they break the publique peace; so that I retract the foresaid distinction, as suspecting it of errour, and distinguish sinners, that they are either against the light of Nature, as tumults, whoredome, drunkennesse, theft; or against the light of faith, as pride, covetousnesse, unbeliefe, schisme, heresie, &c. the former belongs to the Magistrate to punish, the latter belong to the respective churches to censure, and not to the Magistrate to meddle with: and for sins against the light of the Nations, I retract the same as being utterly uncertaine, that the Magistrate hath any such power, yea I do thinke the Magistrate hath no power, as he is a Magistrate, in or about matters of religious worship, but onely to preserve the peace, that no man be molested in or about his worship.[18]

Blackwood's concern, and likely the cause of the tension evident in his previous work, is that genuine disturbances of the peace and destruction to persons or property do not go unpunished by the civil authorities in the name of "freedom". This of course carries with it complications that add further tension, as we have seen a disturbance of the peace could mean the sound of Jews

---

[15] Blackwood, *Storming of Antichrist*, 23.
[16] Blackwood, *Storming of Antichrist*, 25.
[17] Cf. John Coffey, "Puritanism and Liberty Revisited: The Case for Toleration in the English Revolution," *Historical Journal* 41, No. 4 (December, 1998): 966-967.
[18] Ch. Blackwood, *Apostolicall baptisme: or, A sober rejoinder, to a treatise written by Mr. Thomas Blake; intituled, Infants baptisme freed from Antichristianisme*... (London, 1645), 82-83.

singing, or Roman Catholics administering the mass in a private chapel, or Baptists preaching in a hired hall, or having a chat over coffee about the intersection of faith and life. Nonetheless, people should not be allowed to do absolutely anything under the name of "religious liberty", but they should be allowed to practise their faith in peace, and there should be no attempts to coercively establish Christ's Kingdom on Earth. Blackwood cannot then be used to demonstrate that Particular Baptist views on liberty deviated significantly from those of the General Baptists, as they shared the same concerns.

William Kiffen, Particular Baptist Pastor (1612–1702), Unknown Artist

14
Thomas Collier

A prominent signatory of the 1644/1646 Confession, and the only one other than Hanserd Knollys to also later sign the 1677/1689 Confession, is William Kiffen. A group was sent out from John Spilsbury's congregation to plant the Devonshire Square Baptist Church, and Kiffen was elected to serve as pastor, in which role he remained for around sixty years until his death in 1701.[1] He was orphaned as a child of nine, began work as a glover's apprentice at thirteen, and eventually became one of the wealthiest men of his day, using his position and possessions together along with his loyalty to the king (an often repeated though possibly apocryphal story from his life involves King Charles II asking him for a loan of £40,000 and Kiffen deciding to *give* him £10,000[2]) to work for the blessing and benefit of Baptist churches, including freedom for those suffering religious persecution.[3] His ministry spans Monarchy, Republic, and Restoration Eras. His life was marked not only by success but also suffering: he would mourn the death of three adult sons (one of whom was poisoned by a Roman Catholic priest in Venice), a daughter, his wife, as well as two grandsons whom he raised as his own after their father died—William and Benjamin Hewling were executed at the ages of nineteen and twenty-two for their participation in the Monmouth Rebellion of 1685. While a successful businessman and statesman (among other roles, Kiffen served as an MP for Middlesex in 1656) Kiffen was an influential London Baptist pastor and together with John Spilsbury and Hanserd Knollys, was active in encouraging Particular Baptist church planting and evangelism across the nation.

---

[1] James L. Garrett, *Baptist Theology* (Macon: Mercer University Press, 2009), 65.

[2] Ronald A. Johnson, "The Peculiar Ventures of Particular Baptist Pastor William Kiffen and King Charles II of England," *Baptist History and Heritage* 44, No. 1 (winter, 2009): 69.

[3] For more on the life of William Kiffen, see Michael A.G. Haykin, *Kiffen, Knollys, and Keach: Rediscovering our English Baptist Heritage* (Peterborough, ON: H&E Publishing, 2019); Michael A. G. Haykin, *The British Particular Baptists 1638-1910*, Vol. 1 (Springfield: Particular Baptist Press, 1998); Larry Kreitzer, *William Kiffen and his World (Part 5)*, Re-sourcing Baptist History: Seventeenth Century Series Vols. 1-6 (Regent's Park College: Oxford, 2010-2017); and B. A. Ramsbottom, *Stranger than Fiction: the Life of William Kiffin* (Harpenden: Gospel Standard Trust Publications, 1989).

Thomas Collier

One of the evangelists sent out from Kiffen's church in the 1640s was Thomas Collier who served quite effectively as a Baptist pioneer in unreached counties across England, especially as time went on in the West Country, particularly his native Somerset.[4] Thomas Edwards, a Presbyterian who stridently opposed Collier in his early days, said of him in 1646 he "goes about Surrey, Hampshire, and those Counties thereabouts, preaching and dipping."[5] Collier carried out a somewhat apostolic ministry, going on evangelistic tours in cities and counties across the country, quickly baptising new converts and gathering them into churches that would identify from their number suitable leaders. He would then move on, and repeat the process. In this way, not least due to his ministry, the Particular Baptist movement grew rapidly in some places, and flourished in counties where Collier had most influence.[6]

In 1646, Collier published *The Exaltation of Christ in the Dayes of the Gospel*. This work is relevant to many threads of Particular Baptist theology—not least of which being religious liberty—and included a preface by Particular Baptist Leader and signatory of the 1646 revision of the 1644 Confession, Hanserd Knollys. In it, Collier demonstrates that if Christ really is *the alone High-Priest, Prophet, and King, of Saints* found in the subtitle, there should be no system of coercion into a national church.

It seems to Collier that much of the framework for faulty systems of church and state relations such as Erastianism and Presbyterianism lie in confusion of different, if connected, things: Old and New Covenants, Israel and the Church, Abraham's seed by birth (Jews) and Abraham's spiritual seed by re-birth in Christ (Christians), physical penalties in Israel and spiritual penalties in the church, circumcision of male infants born and baptism of all believers reborn, and so on and so forth.[7] Besides these theological issues, there is the

---

[4] Garrett, *Baptist Theology*, 80-83; James M. Renihan, "Confessing the Faith in 1644 and 1689," *Reformed Baptist Theological Review* 3, No. 1 (January, 2006): 27-47; James M. Renihan, "Thomas Collier's Descent Into Error: Collier, Calvinism, and the Second London Confession," *Reformed Baptist Theological Review* 1, No. 1 (January, 2004): 67-84; James M. Renihan, "The Strange Case of Thomas Collier," *Journal of the Institute of Reformed Baptist Studies* 3, No. 1 (November, 2016): 97-122.

[5] Thomas Edwards, *The Second Part of Gangraena: Or a Catalog and Discovery of many of the Errours, Heresies, Blasphemies, and pernicious Practices of the Sectaries of this time* (London, 1646), 148.

[6] Richard Dale Land, "Doctrinal Controversies of English Particular Baptists (1644-1691) as Illustrated by the Career and Writings of Thomas Collier" (D.Phil. diss., University of Oxford, 1979), 29.

[7] Thomas Collier, *The Exaltation of Christ in the Dayes of the Gospel: as the alone High-Priest, Prophet, and King, of Saints* (London, 1646), 94-97; 162-163; 223.

practical matter of what persecutors are doing: taking upon themselves the authoritative position of Christ over sinners in judgement.

> The most great and learned men in the World at this day rage against the Kingdom of Christ, they would set up a kingdome of their own, and then compell men unto it: whoever it is that establishes a Worship with Lawes and Edicts, to compell all unto it, and to inflict bodily punishments, upon all that refuse it, or cannot joyne with it, doth what in him lyeth absolutely to destroy the Kingdome of Christ; over the soul: and if men be erroneous and worship contrary to the rule of the Truth it is Christ himself that must judge him, and not man *he* (to whit, God) *hath committed all judgement to the Son.*[8]

He later reiterates that it is a worldly, even satanic, mindset to attempt establishing Christ's spiritual reign over his saints by physical, violent means. The alternative he proposes? "Let men turne the world into Church by preaching as fast as they can, or as Christ will."[9]

It is not that Collier doubts the power of the gospel or the supremacy of Christ—rather he believes in it so much so that he trusts it to be sufficient to speak for and commend itself to a lost and broken world. The message is compelling in itself: methods of compulsion are not needed and if used will not "turne the world into Church" but if anything turn Church into the world, as it becomes a social instead of a spiritual body, filled with unregenerate people of insincere faith and ineffective practice.

In the tumultuous days of the Republic, some of Collier's views and emphases shift inconsistently to the extent that some have thought there were two Thomas Colliers writing on similar subjects at the same time but with varied conclusions.[10] This apparent double-mindedness was indicative of deeper problems that increasingly began to surface, as the years passed, but were not always easy to pin down. Some matters Collier himself would admit and repent of: there was a fairly early season in which he questioned the accuracy, authority, and sufficiency of Scripture, which would be held against him even after he had returned to the orthodoxy of the First London Confession. There were also concerns that Collier spoke of Christ in terms that seemed to indicate less than full deity, and he denied the eternal generation of the Son, which some

---

[8] Collier, *The Exaltation of Christ*, 222.
[9] Collier, *The Exaltation of Christ*, 239.
[10] Land, "Doctrinal Controversies," 33.

interpreted (incorrectly) as Collier denying the eternity of the Son. There is sufficient evidence from the 1650s, however, that Collier addressed these quirks to his own and his peers' satisfaction. One area where he remained consistent was his ecclesiology, and with that his distinctively Baptist understanding of religious liberty.

Controversy exploded in 1674, when Collier published *The Body of Divinity*, followed two years later by an *Additional Word to the Body of Divinity*. It had been 15 years since Collier's last published work, and how long he had subscribed to some of the views he developed is unclear. In any case, his beliefs were plain for all to read, and sufficiently concerning that a process of associational examination, engagement, and discipline was enacted by concerned churches and their leaders. Historic Christian doctrine and important distinctives of Protestant, reformational belief were rejected, particularly with regard to Christology, soteriology, and eschatology. Nehemiah Coxe wrote a response in 1677: *Vindiciæ veritatis, or, A confutation—the heresies and gross errours asserted by Thomas Collier in his additional word to his body of divinity*. In its introductory comments, Collier is identified as walking "very frequently" in the steps of "Pelagians, Jesuits, and Socinians" and "doth transcend the Heresies of those mentioned." A prefatory note to the reader discloses that there had been problems behind the scenes with Collier for "many years," but that repentance was looked for and sometimes seemed to appear, only for Collier ultimately to persist in error. While Coxe is author of the book, he did so not out of personal inclination, but "by the joint and earnest persuasion of several of the Elders," six of whom signed the prefatory note as an endorsement of the book's critiques. The first name listed is the pastor of Collier's sending church, William Kiffen.[11]

Associating Particular Baptist churches and their leaders were left with no other option than to reject Collier, and those who agreed with him.[12] While the changes of the decades since the First London Confession were significant and represented sufficient cause for an updated treatment of Particular Baptist belief, it was Collier's defection that proved to be a significant catalyst in moving towards a new confession.[13]

---

[11] Nehemiah Coxe, "Christian Reader", in *Vindiciæ veritatis, or, A confutation - the heresies and gross errours asserted by Thomas Collier in his additional word to his body of divinity* (London, 1677).

[12] Mark R. Bell, *Apocalypse How?: Baptist Movements during the English Revolution* (Macon: Mercer, 2000),142-143; for more on this see Renihan, "Thomas Collier's Descent", 67-84.

[13] Haykin, *Kiffin, Keach, and Knollys*, 68.

Detail from Londini Angliae regni metropolis delineatio accuratissima, F. de Witt, 1693

15
The Second London Baptist Confession

As previously discussed, the end of Cromwell's Protectorate and the Restoration of the monarchy under Charles II in 1660 led to the Corporation Act (1661), the Act of Uniformity (1662), the Conventicle Act (1664), the Five-Mile Act (1665), and the Test Act (1673), all of which were laws designed to suppress Non-conformists and Dissenters while strengthening the established church.[1] At the same time, victims of the new legislations were growing in cooperation with members of other ecclesiological convictions. This is most evident in Presbyterian-Baptist relations. As one historian writes: "When Presbyterians, who had provided the chief stimuli for outbursts either for or against religious liberty in the 1640's, decided to try to live with other groups they removed a great deal of motivation for writings on the subject."[2] The Baptists, as a result, were no longer swift to label Presbyterians as "Antichrist." Instead, Baptist leaders such as Benjamin Keach penned words like these:

> Can English Protestants, who do profess
> To serve one God in Truth and Holiness,
> Slight all my wishes and requests despise?
> O! Hearken to my counsel, and be wise,
> Let Wrathful Pride, and foolish Self-conceit
> Let Quibbles and Sophisticated deceit,
> Be quite exploded: let a cool Debate
> All Fundamentals of Religion state:
> In such you all will certainly agree:
> (O happy Model of sweet Unity!)
> Let none that to those Principles do stick
> Be branded with name of Heretick;
> It glads my heart to hear 'em call each other
> By that sweet title of a Christian Brother.[3]

---

[1] James L. Garrett, *Baptist Theology* (Macon: Mercer University Press, 2009), 71.
[2] Leon McBeth, *English Baptist Literature on Religious Liberty to 1689* (New York: Arno, 1980), 149.
[3] Benjamin Keach, *Sion in distress: or, The groans of the Protestant Church* (London, 1681), 33.

It seems then that the Aristotelian saying is right: a common danger unites even the bitterest enemies. In conjunction with these improved relations, the group of Particular Baptists that drew up the Second London Confession in 1677 in many ways as part of their response to the Collier crisis, used the Presbyterians' Westminster Confession (1647) as their starting point, adapting it to reflect Baptist principles. Often, Westminster is followed verbatim, but one significant area in which the Baptist Confession differs from the Presbyterian confession is the matter of religious liberty.

The first clear evidence of this difference is the deletion of Westminster's Chapter Twenty, paragraph four from the equivalent Baptist portion, Chapter Twenty-one. It reads:

> And, for their publishing of such opinions, or maintaining of such practices, as are contrary to the light of nature, or to the known principles of Christianity (whether concerning faith, worship, or conversation), or to the power of godliness; or, such erroneous opinions or practices, as either in their own nature, or in the manner of publishing or maintaining them, are destructive to the external peace and order which Christ has established in the Church, they may lawfully be called to account, and proceeded against, by the censures of the Church, and by the power of the civil magistrate.[4]

It has been argued that this statement does not advocate civil action "against unlawful *opinions* but only destructive *actions* affecting external peace and order."[5] If this be the case why does the document speak quite clearly of "opinions"? Given Baptist loyalty to the king in lawful civil affairs, and their opposition to treason, terrorism, and "destructive actions," why is the paragraph missing from their confession? The Baptists were not alone in recognising a threat to religious liberty in this paragraph; the Congregationalists had deleted it as well in their Savoy Declaration (1658).[6] Why? "They rejected the idea that the state had the right to punish men for publicly teaching heresy."[7]

---

[4] G. I. Williamson, *The Westminster Confession of Faith for Study Classes*, 2nd ed. (Phillipsburg: P&R Publishing, 2004), 200-201.

[5] Williamson, *The Westminster Confession*, 200-201.

[6] Samuel E. Waldron, *A Modern Exposition of the 1689 Baptist Confession of Faith*, 3rd ed. (Darlington; reprint, with a new preface, Evangelical Press, 2005), 256.

[7] Waldron, *A Modern Exposition*, 256.

Every Man's Conscience

Another significant alteration to Westminster is found in London's Chapter Twenty-four, on the subject of the civil magistrate. Paragraph two of Westminster's Chapter Twenty-three tells us that the civil magistrate is "to maintain piety" as well as justice and peace and paragraph three tells us that the civil magistrate,

> hath authority, and it is his duty, to take order that unity and peace be preserved in the Church, that the truth of God be kept pure and entire, that all blasphemies and heresies be suppressed, all corruptions and abuses in worship and discipline prevented or reformed, and all the ordinances of God duly settled, administered, and observed. For the better effecting whereof, he hath power to call synods, to be present at them and to provide that whatsoever is transacted in them be according to the mind of God.

The reference to maintaining piety is absent from the London Confession, and all trace of Westminster's paragraph 3 has vanished. By their silence, the Particular Baptists were communicating the belief held from their inception that it was not the duty of civil authorities to make laws pertaining to religion, nor indeed to enforce the "first table of the law." Civil rulers are given the task of punishing evil and rewarding good as Romans 13 relates, but given the textual context (which makes reference only to the second table of the Law) and the historical context (pagan Rome), the evil of which Paul speaks cannot be of a religious nature.[8]

Particular Baptists and General Baptists did not let their divergent views on the extent of the atonement distract from fundamental agreement on foundational realities of church identity and kingdom mission. The General Baptist's *An Orthodox Creed* followed the 1677 Confession very similarly in its article on "The Civil Magistrate," and begins almost identically with an emphasis on the sovereignty of God and the boundaries of government:

> The Supreme Lord and King of all the World, hath ordained Civil Magistrates (Romans 13.1,2,3,4. Prov. 8.15) to be under Him, over the People for his own Glory, and the Publick Good. And the Office of a Magistrate, may be accepted of, and executed by Christians, when lawfully called thereunto (1 Pet. 2.14, Prov. 20.26); and God hath given the

---

[8] Waldron, *A Modern Exposition*, 296-297.

power of the Sword into the hands of all lawful Magistrates, for the defence and incouragement of them that do well, and for the Punishment of evil-doers (1 Pet. 2.14, Prov. 20.26), and for the maintenance of Justice, and Peace, according to the wholesome Laws of each Kingdom, and Commonwealth (2 Sam.23.3. Psal. 82:3, 4. & 72:4, 7).[9]

Lest any notion of governance "for the publick good" lead to creeping government interference with—or coercion of—religious practice, both the 1677 confession and the 1679 creed include clear statements on liberty. According to the 1677 confession, the worship of God is one of "yielding obedience unto Him, not out of slavish fear, (Luk 1:73-75; 1Jo 4:18), but a child-like love and willing mind."[10] It continues by highlighting the freedom of human conscience:

God alone is (Jam 4:12; Rom 14:4) Lord of the conscience, and hath left it free from the doctrines and commandments of men (Act 4:19; 5:29; 1Co 7:23; Mat 15:9;) which are in any thing contrary to his Word, or not contained in it. So that to believe such doctrines, or obey such commands out of conscience, (Col 2:20,22-23) is to betray true liberty of conscience; and the requiring of an (1Co 3:5; 2Co 1:24) implicit faith, an absolute and blind obedience, is to destroy liberty of conscience and reason also.[11]

The principles of the 1677 confession are expanded on in the 1679 creed, but remain in essence, with the helpful additional clarification: "no pretended good end whatsoever, by any Man, can make that Action, Obedience, or Practice, lawful and good, that is not grounded in, or upon the Authority of holy Scripture, or right Reason agreeable thereunto."[12] In other words, even claims that something is for "the publick good" must be weighed against Scripture or at least reason in the conscience.

Whatever new-found cooperation Baptists might have had with Presbyterians, it did not alter their consistent belief in the liberty to preach, publish, and practise religion as directed by conscience, without state interference. Baptists

---

[9] Thomas Monck et al., *An Orthodox creed, or, A Protestant confession of faith: being an essay to unite and confirm all true Protestants in the fundamental articles of the Christian religion, against the errors and heresies of the church of Rome* (London, 1679), Article 45.

[10] *The Baptist Confession of Faith With Scripture Proofs Adopted by the Ministers and Messengers of the General Assembly Which Met in London* (London, 1689), 22:1.

[11] *The Baptist Confession of Faith*, 22:2.

[12] Monck et al., *An Orthodox Creed*, Article 46.

continued to maintain the conviction that people can only enter the covenant family of believers by spiritual regeneration with graciously given repentance and faith in Christ, in response to the power of the Holy Spirit in the preaching of the Word. The Kingdom of Christ would always be different from the kingdoms of this world, and the only sword the church should wield is the sword of the Spirit, the word of God. Regardless of the friendliness or hostility of the government and its policies to their faith and practice, Baptists would keep preaching, "dipping" those credibly professing repentance and faith in Christ, and voluntarily assembling when and where they could, openly or secretly, in the faith that Christ would build his church, and the gates of hell would not prevail against it.

Portrait of James II of England, Godfrey Kneller

16
Liberty?

Persecution under the reign of Charles II continued to intensify and endured beyond the death of Charles and the accession of his brother James II to the throne in 1685, such that the years 1660–1688 are known as "the Great Persecution." Hercules Collins, a successor to John Spilsbury at the church in Wapping, described the situation after the death in prison of Seventh-Day Baptist Francis Bampfield and "Zachariah Ralpshon" (an alias for Jeremiah Marsden, whose funeral at Bunhill Fields reportedly drew around 5000 people):

> God gave the People into their Enemies Hand, but they shewed them no Mercy: Upon the Ancients hast thou heavily laid the Yoke: (as now Men of threescore, fourscore Years of Age, hurried to Prison for nothing else but for Worshiping their God; and how do many in the Exercise of their Power weary themselves in contriving against the Innocent, in sitting in Judgment against them, from morning until nine or ten a Clok at night, and then hurry them to Prison, Old and Young, Male and Female, Bond and Free, Poor and Rich.[1]

William Kiffen later reflected on "the Temptations some were under" during Charles II and the early days of James II's reign:

> their Lives being in their Enemies Hands; the great Sufferings, by Imprisonments, Excommunications, etc. that did attend from the Ecclesiastical Courts, as also by the frequent Molestations of Informers against our Meetings, by means whereof many Families were ruined in their Estates, as also deprived of all our Liberties, and denied the common Justice of the Nation, by the Oaths and Perjury of the vilest of Mankind.[2]

---

[1] Hercules Collins, *Counsel for the living, occasioned from the dead, or, A discourse on Job III, 17, 18 arising from the deaths of Mr. Fran. Bampfield and Mr. Zach. Ralphson* (London, 1684), 15.

[2] Arnold H. J. Baines, "Innocency Vindicated; or, Reproach Wip'd Off," *The Baptist Quarterly* 16, No. 4 (1955): 165.

Liberty?

The accession of James II was widely welcomed, and somewhat celebrated for the peaceful transition of power. There was, however, a contender to the throne. Charles II had no legitimate heirs, but at least fourteen children by various mistresses from the age of eighteen. His eldest son was born in Rotterdam to Lucy Walter: James Scott, first duke of Monmouth. Monmouth, who had been in exile in the Dutch Republic since 1679 due to his growing popularity as a military officer, landed at Dorset and gathering an army of disaffected people—socio-economic commoners and religious Dissenters—marched toward battle:

> all the boundaries of the Government have of late been broken, & nothing left unattempted for turning our *limited Monarchy* into an *absolute Tyranny*. For such hath been the transactions of affaires within this Nation for severall Years last past, that tho the *Protestant Religion, & Libertyes* of the people, were fenced & hedg'd about, by as many *Laws*, as the Wisdome of men could devise, for their preservation against *Popery* and *Arbitrary Power;* our *Religion* hath been all a long undermined by *Popish Councells,* and our *Priviledges* ravished from us by fraud & violence. And more especially, the whole course & series of the Life of the present *Usurper,* hath been but one continued conspiracy against the *Reformed Religion,* & rights of the *Nation*.[3]

For all his ambition, military experience, and claim to the throne, Monmouth had no viable strategy. His makeshift army of men armed with available weaponry and improvised farm tools was soundly defeated at the Battle of Sedgemoor, July 6, 1685. A malnourished Monmouth, disguised as a shepherd, was captured in the ditch of a pea field. He was executed on July 15, 1685 at the hands of executioner Jack Ketch, who was infamous for botched executions: Monmouth asked Ketch to behead him in one blow, Ketch obliged him by taking five, then sawing with a knife before the head was successfully severed.[4] Around 1300 were tried in what would become known as "the Bloody Assizes": 320 or so would be executed, including William Kiffen's grandsons, the Hewling brothers, and 800 were transported to forced labour in Barbados.

---

[3] James Scott, duke of Monmouth, *The declaration of James Duke of Monmouth, & the noblemen, gentlemen & others, now in arms, for defence & vindication of the Protestant religion, & the laws, rights, & privilieges of England, from the invasion made upon them, & for delivering the kingdom from the usurpation & tyranny of James Duke of York* (London: n.p., 1685).

[4] William Tait and Christian Isobel Johnstone eds., "The Life and Rebellion of the Duke of Monmouth," *Tait's Edinburgh Magazine* (January 1845): 50-60.

Such brutal scenes would not instil confidence in any change of policy towards toleration. James continued to clumsily pursue what appeared to be a biased agenda in favour of his fellow Roman Catholics. Considering the history of religious totalitarianism under the Roman Catholic Church, the increasing promotion to and prominence of Roman Catholics in places of power was not reassuring. When an initially supportive parliament did not fall in line with James' efforts to extend toleration to Roman Catholics, he proved many suspicions right by continuously proroguing parliament for a year and a half from November 1685 before dissolving it all together in 1687.[5]

As a Roman Catholic monarch facing an Anglican establishment, perhaps James felt that as a dissenter from the religio-political status quo, he had more in common with Protestant Non-conformists and Dissenters than might immediately meet the eye. A loosening of restrictions came in the form of royal patents that could be purchased, exempting them from the consequences of violating the penal laws in the past and future. Charles II had granted these to people who were reportedly loyal to the Royalist cause in the days of civil war and the Republic, and James extended them liberally upon request to those who promised to conduct themselves peaceably towards his government. Some Baptists, like Nehemiah Coxe, did this without any strain of conscience: it brought much needed relief. Others, like William Kiffen—experienced in business and politics, but also grieving the loss of his grandsons—would resume public meetings without requesting such a patent or recognising the king's authority to give it; liberty to worship was not the king's to take, and it followed that it was not his to give.[6]

On April 4, 1687 in the absence of a functioning parliament, James delivered what Non-conformists had been longing for: a Declaration of Indulgence, suspending penal laws against all Non-conformists. It represented a remarkable turnaround from the persecutions inflicted by Charles II and the punishments meted out in the early days of James' reign.

> We cannot but heartily wish, as it will easily be believed, that all the people of our dominions were members of the Catholic Church. Yet we humbly thank Almighty God, it is and has of long time been our constant sense and opinion (which upon divers occasions we have declared) that conscience ought not to be constrained nor people forced in matters of

---

[5] For a thorough classical analysis of the reign of James II, see Thomas Babbington Macauley, *The History of England from the Accession of James II*, Vols. 1-2 (London: Folio Society, 2009).

[6] Baines, "Innocency Vindicated", 165.

mere religion; it has ever been directly contrary to our inclination, as we think it is to the interest of government, which it destroys by spoiling trade, depopulating countries, and discouraging strangers, and finally, that it never obtained the end for which it was employed. And in this we are the more confirmed by the reflections we have made upon the conduct of the four last reigns. For after all the frequent and pressing endeavours that were used in each of them to reduce this kingdom to an exact conformity in religion, it is visible the success has not answered the design, and that the difficulty is invincible.

The decree went on to promise free exercise of religion "without any molestation or disturbance whatsoever." Penalties for not attending church, not receiving the Sacrament, or for any other expression of religious non-conformity were suspended, and previously illegal religious gatherings were promised protection:

And that all our subjects may enjoy such their religious assemblies with greater assurance and protection, we have thought it requisite, and do hereby command, that no disturbance of any kind be made or given unto them, under pain of our displeasure, and to be further proceeded against with the uttermost severity.[7]

Furthermore, religious oaths to the Church of England would no longer be required for civil or military office. The progressive new policy would be enforced across the nation's local authorities by a small interdenominational team of regulators. The group was led by the Quaker William Penn, but eleven of the fifteen men—almost seventy-five percent—were Particular Baptists including Collier-critic and 1677 confession co-editor Nehemiah Coxe and coffee house pastor James Jones.[8]

But there was a problem. James II had no constitutional mandate or parliamentary support. The declaration was made by James II according to the old pre-Republic assumption of the divine right of kings, as by an absolute monarch. James' declaration of indulgence represented liberty, but by tyranny.

---

[7] Andrew Browning, "Declaration of Indulgence of King James II, April 4, 1687," *English Historical Documents* 8 (London: Eyre and Spottiswoode, 1953): 399–400.

[8] Matthew James Gray, "'Baptism, No Wall of Division': Seventeenth-Century Particular Baptists and Dynamics of Toleration" (D.Phil. thesis, University of Adelaide, 2018), 244; for more on the subject, see Scott Sowerby, *Making Toleration: The Repealers and the Glorious Revolution* (Cambridge, MA: Harvard University Press, 2013).

Ironically, by requiring that his declaration be read publicly in the Church of England, James imposed himself on ecclesiastical life and so undermined the message of his declaration. Seven bishops refused to read the declaration in their worship gatherings, and they were imprisoned. James' daughter Mary, married to the Protestant William of Orange, was displaced from the line of succession by the birth of a son. James seemed to be stacking Roman Catholic allies in positions of civil and military authority, and was growing a professional army, under his command, in peacetime. These events created substantial unrest and fears of a Roman Catholic dynasty and with it, religious coercion. In 1688, a large army—this time invited, organised, and equipped—landed in England from the Dutch Republic, led by the Protestant William of Orange—James' son-in-law. Unlike Monmouth a mere few years before, there was little to no resistance put up against William's force, and James II fled the country, disguised as a woman.

The new King William III's Act of Toleration in 1688 extended liberty to Non-conformists, but there were qualifications, and the Act was a far cry from the universal vision of the Baptists, momentarily achieved, oddly enough, by the absolutist decree of a Roman Catholic monarch. It must be asked though whether progress under James—a solitary man acting in his own authority with assumed power, outside of due process—had really been made at all. William Kiffen did not believe so. In 1689, enjoying their new freedoms, messengers representing over 100 Particular Baptist churches from across England and Wales gathered for several days in a large meeting room at Broken Wharfe, on the Thames River in London. The most famous outcome of that assembly was the formal adoption of the 1677 Second London Confession of Faith, revised in 1688—it would thereby become more popularly known by the year 1689. Another outcome was a document clearing the record: rumours that Baptists were complicit in monarchical totalitarianism were untrue, and the few individuals who had unwisely been used by James II had been dealt with:

> To the utmost of our Knowledg, there was not one Congregation that had a Hand, or gave Consent to any thing of that Nature, nor did ever countenance any of their Members to own an Absolute Power in the. late King, to dispense with the Penal Laws and Tests; being well satis-

Liberty?

fied, that the doing thereof by his sole Prerogative, would lay the Foundation of Destruction of the Protestant Religion, and Slavery to this Kingdom.[9]

In which case, in might be said then, that the 1689 Act was not a step back but some authentic progress was made. Some liberty was achieved, and future liberties would be built on this foundation—but properly, even if incrementally. But that liberty was social, granted or not according to the laws of the nation. Baptists maintained that whatever the status of religious liberty in the statute books or social life of the United Kingdom, they already had soul liberty according to the scriptural books of Christ's Kingdom.

---

[9] Baines, "Innocency Vindicated," 164.

Conclusion

Many professing Christians in the West are not sure how to face the exchange of cultural Christianity for cultural paganism, or how to live peaceful and quiet lives, with distinctively held and openly shared convictions, in a more religiously diverse context than they or their ancestors had grown accustomed to. At the same time, they are shaped by personal experiences and catechised more by various forms of reactionary media than by the Scriptures, the fellowship of believers, and the history of the church, and so are characterised by outrage instead of sobriety, compassion, and perseverance in doing good. Some respond by adjusting "the faith that was once for all delivered to the saints" to fit with their own ideas, and others leave the faith altogether. Others are totally committed, and if they had had their way, would pugilistically insist that others be too—betraying, perhaps, a different kind of insecurity.

This social and spiritual rootlessness has led many who maintain orthodox Christian faith to seek more than the superficialities of a broad, ill-defined, and increasingly politicised evangelicalism or even the soteriology-centric coalitions of the early twenty-first century. Theological and ecclesiological retrieval, where it occurs, is resulting in Baptists becoming more "Baptist", Presbyterians becoming more "Presbyterian", and so forth. As a result, new conversations are beginning, which may be found to not be so new at all.

In *The Case for Christian Nationalism*, for example, Stephen Wolfe makes arguments that would not have been at all out of place from England's mid-seventeenth-century Anglicans and Presbyterians—or even Roman Catholics for that matter. In doing so, he makes the following observation about the incompatibility of Baptist theology with anything like the system he himself promotes:

> pedobaptism (i.e., infant baptism) is the position most natural to Christian nationalism, for baptizing infants brings them outwardly (at least) into the people of God. When the body politic is baptized, all are people of God ... But credobaptism likely creates problems for Christian nationalism. It is no accident that Baptists tend to be advocates for near

Conclusion

absolute religious liberty, and this is not only due to their tradition of dissent. Their theology of baptism restricts Christian obligation to the credobaptized, and thus the mass of society, at least in people's formative years, do not (in principle) have Christian obligations. It is difficult to see how cultural Christianity, as I've described it, could operate effectively with that theology. Pedobaptism is consistent with Christian nationalism because it makes possible a society that is baptized in infancy and thus is subject to Christian demands for all of life.[1]

While I shall leave it to paedobaptist brothers and sisters to dispute the connection of paedobaptism to Christian nationalism, I do believe a historical case can be made for its greater compatibility with or abuse for religiously coercive systems. This was early English Baptist's experience from all paedobaptist denominations. Greater catholicity had developed by the 1680s, but Baptists' fundamentally different ecclesiology and distinctive covenant theology continued to leave them ostracised in English, European, and colonial American life.

Christopher Blackwood wrote, "The testimony of a few that are not blinded with temporall ends, but swim painfully against the stream, is not to be slighted."[2] The early English Baptists, both General and Particular, swam painfully against the stream of their day to plead theologically and pragmatically for religious liberty that extended to all people. They acknowledged that the civil authorities should judge all who plot or carry out destruction to property and person, who transgress the dictates of natural law infused in creation by God, and should not be naïve about some people taking advantage of "liberty" to do so. It is not the civil authority's responsibility, however, to meddle with matters of religion, to coerce people to or away from any faith, or to sponsor a "church". For the Baptists, there could be no legitimate national "Church of England" or anywhere else for that matter but only visible local churches of Christ; people do not become citizens of heaven in accord with the geographical location of their earth-bound existence, and physical birth is a separate event from rebirth with repentance and faith in Christ.

---

[1] Stephen Wolfe, *The Case for Christian Nationalism* (Moscow: Canon Press, 2022), 217-218. I hope, my agreement with Wolfe's conclusion regarding Baptist incompatibility with Christian nationalism aside, it will be clear to the reader from my comments here that this is in no way, shape, form, or fashion, an endorsement of this book or the wider project it represents.

[2] Christopher Blackwood, *Storming of Antichrist in his two last and strongest Garrisons, of Compulsion of Conscience and Infants Baptisme...* (London, 1644), 3.

It is sometimes argued that the Baptist defence of religious liberty sprang from the Arminianism of the General Baptists, and that the Particular Baptists therefore must have had a different take on the issue, with a view allegedly drawn more from Calvinism.[3] The evidence says otherwise. General and Particular Baptists frequently use the same arguments against persecution, including proper spheres of authority, the identity of the church, the nature of Christ's Kingdom, the possibility of eleventh-hour conversions, and scriptural proofs such as Jesus' parable of the tares (Matt. 13:24–30, 36–43). Additionally, the General Baptist Orthodox Creed (1679) uses similar, sometimes exact, wording as the 1677 London Confession to address matters of liberty and the civil authorities.[4] It was not Arminianism or Calvinism that defined Baptist views on religious liberty, but a simple desire to follow the Bible's teaching, whatever advantages or disadvantages may come.[5]

In 1688, a second edition of the Second London Confession was published. A year later it was adopted by the first assembly of English Particular Baptists. Earlier in that same year, 1689, the Act of Toleration was passed, granting on the British Isles greater levels of liberty than previously known, paving the way forward for future laws.[6] The vast contributions of the early English Baptists, a representative sample of which we have introduced, were vital in bringing this and later freedoms to pass.

Charles Spurgeon wrote in March 1873, in *The Sword and Trowel*, "We will go on with our spiritual duties quietly enough if those in power will deal out equal measure to all religions." He went further and said, "Till every man of every faith shall be equal before the eyes of the law as to his religious rights, we cannot, and dare not, cease to be political."[7]

By so doing, Spurgeon was not breaking with Christian orthodoxy to espouse a relativistic religious universalism, or a pluralistic religious humanism, affirming the legitimacy of other faiths as acceptable and effective ways to God. His message was firmly that of Scripture, that Jesus is "the way, the truth, and the life" apart from whom no one can come to the Heavenly Father

---

[3] Stoddard, "Seventeenth Century Particular Baptist Views", for example.

[4] Ian Randall, "Early English Baptists and Religious Liberty," *Anabaptism Today*, No. 4 (October, 1993).

[5] Ian Randall, "Baptists, The Gospel and Freedom of Conscience," in *50th Anniversary Lecture of the SBHS* (Dunstable: Fauconberg Press, 2010), 12-13.

[6] James L. Garrett, *Baptist Theology* (Macon: Mercer University Press, 2009), 72.

[7] C. H. Spurgeon, *The Sword and Trowel: 1873* (London: Passmore & Alabaster, 1873), 45-48.

Conclusion

(John 14:6). Rather, he was trusting in the word of God, not a weaponised government, to do the work of gospel advance and to shape the conscience of the nation. He was trusting the efficacy of the one Lord who gives and calls to one faith and ordains one baptism, and the sufficiency of the preached gospel to save repentant hearers without coercive human aid. In "A blast of the trumpet against false peace", Spurgeon makes this quite clear: "No state has any right to dictate what religion I shall believe; but nevertheless there is a true gospel and there are thousands of false ones."[8]

One does not have to look far to see threats to the principle of universal religious liberty, from internet trolls to more credible efforts in the corridors of power, across the political spectrum. At the same time, the political weaponisation of freely practiced religion to various ends that genuinely endanger the peace and security of a nation and its citizens is also a threat to universal religious liberty, abusing and perverting liberty at the expense of others and putting legal protections to the test. For many people around the world, the notion of religious liberty - including though not limited to that of Christians[9] — is a dream, and believers are forced to find creative, risky ways to privately and communally practise their faith and proclaim their message with no meaningful assurances of safety whatsoever.

The Baptist approach to religious liberty and what it means more broadly for life even in hostile environments does not promise ease or even safety. But it is not shaped by circumstantial complaints—rather scriptural convictions as to the nature of Christ's Kingdom, and how that overflows into how we treat people others may be frightened of or prejudiced against.

For all of his peaceful living and diplomacy, there came a day when a septuagenarian Roger Williams stood in the middle of a street reasoning with the leaders of a coalition of marauding Natives, as the settlement he had founded went up in flames and his own house burned behind him: "Why...? This Hous of mine now burning before mine Eyes hath Lodged kindly Some Thousands of You these Ten Years."[10] He explained the injustice of what they were doing, warned them of the just civil consequences they would face, and urged them to repent of their robberies and murders. Astonishingly, they did not assault

---

[8] C. H. Spurgeon, "A Blast of the Trumpet against False Peace," in *The New Park Street Pulpit Sermons, Vol. 6* (London: Passmore and Alabaster, 1860), 293.

[9] See the annually updated *World Watch List* from Open Doors for a helpful guide to 50 countries where following Christ carries substantial risks.

[10] Glenn W. LaFantasie ed., "The Road to Banishment: Editorial Note," in *The Correspondence of Roger Williams, Vol. I, 1629-1653* (Hanover: Brown University Press, 1988), 722.

Williams himself, and warned him not to go too near the burning houses. A witness to their conversation reported that they "told Mr. Williams that he was a good Man, and been kinde to them formerly, and therefore would not hurt him."[11] Such boldness and grace in the face of attack is the fruit of core principles that frame a liberated life that seeks others' liberty under the civil law, and desires spiritual liberty in Christ for a world at war with God and itself. Williams related those principles in a letter decades earlier, written from the native trading post of Cawcawmsqussick, and we may list them in summary[12]:

> Kiss truth where it may be found.
> Advance justice.
> Seek and make peace, if possible, with all men.
> Secure your own life.

This then is the essence of the Baptist—indeed, New Testament—approach to religious liberty:

> Allow for the existence and free practice of other religions
> or none, according to everyone's conscience.
> Accept adherents to other religious systems or none as
> fellow *imago Dei* bearing humans, and treat them with love,
> care, and respect. This love includes free and fair critique,
> dialogue, debate, and even strong disagreement, but with
> the understanding that faith is a matter for everyone's
> conscience.
> Affirm—whatever the practices of other people or the
> policy of the governing authorities - the exclusive
> confession that only "Jesus is Lord" and the
> inclusive invitation to all people everywhere to repent of
> sin and believe in Jesus for eternal salvation. Whether
> people respond to that confession and invitation or not is a
> matter for everyone's conscience.

---

[11] LaFantasie, *The Correspondence of Roger Williams*, 728 n31.
[12] LaFantasie, *The Correspondence of Roger Williams*, 234.

Acknowledgements

The story of this book began in 2010, when I studied Baptist Heritage under Malcolm Yarnell as part of the Southwestern Baptist Theological Seminary's Oxford Study Program. It was at Dr. Yarnell's encouragement that I pursued, some years later, publishing the present volume. I am grateful to him, Madison Grace, and the students and faculty on that trip, who fuelled my interest in Baptist history and theology and strengthened my resolve to maintain historic Baptist distinctiveness in my own ministry, not for the sake of tradition but faithfulness to Scripture. I am particularly honoured by Dr. Yarnell's provision of a foreword to the present volume. I am also grateful for the hospitality of the Regent's Park College of the University of Oxford, and the Angus Library and Archive.

My studies in Christian history and theology continued at Highland Theological College (University of the Highlands and Islands). While expressing gratitude for that institution more generally, I would like to especially thank church history tutor Nick Needham, and Robert Shillaker who supervised the work out of which this present volume is born. My studies at HTC would not have been possible were it not for the excellent work of the late Martin Cameron, librarian—a kind, gracious, and hospitable man who worked with diligence and care—absent from the body, present with the Lord.

I am grateful for those who over the years have taken an interest in and read various drafts of the present work, some of whom have also provided additional encouragement and feedback: not least Bart Barber, Jason Duesing, Sharon James, Jim Renihan, Andrew King, and Jeremy Walker. Others in the publishing world who read drafts of the book, gave me advice, or arranged for anonymous readers to read and provide feedback are also appreciated, particularly Mike Adams and Thomas Creedy. Thank you too, to Ryan Edwards, who went painstakingly through the manuscript to proof and edit it ready for publication. I am also grateful to Stephen Talas of www.designvst.com for his assistance with the images in the book.

Acknowledgements

Thank you, Chance Faulkner, Michael Haykin, and all involved in the publication process with H&E Publishing: I hope this work is a valuable addition to your growing catalogue, particularly in the sphere of Baptist studies.

To those who have provided endorsements, the time you took to read and commend the present work is greatly appreciated.

The present work would not be possible, considering my own constraints of time, place, and resource, if I did not have the greatest collection of literature in the English language within easy reach. The British Library has made the world of the seventeenth century accessible and affordable, easing the research process. I forgive you for not letting eleven-year-old me have a membership.

I am grateful for the incredibly diverse community in which I live, my friends, neighbours, and acquaintances from the rich array of backgrounds around me, and the church I have the privilege of pastoring, which reflects this diversity—Grace Baptist Church Wood Green. You enrich and sharpen me!

Last but not least, I am grateful for my family. Whether in the United States, Ukraine, or the United Kingdom, dead or alive, in contact or not, there is no me without you, and I want to honour you. Particular honour is due to my parents, Barry and Frances King. Thank you, Dad and Mom, for passing on to me a love of history, literature, and above all a love for the Lord, the lost, and the local church. And to my dear wife Uliana, who at the time of writing this, bears our first child: thank you for your constant support, encouragement, and humouring my excursions to see "interesting" and "important" things like street signs or modern buildings with distant Baptist history connections. In you, I have found a good thing and favour from the Lord.

"Now to him who is able to do far more abundantly than all that we ask or think, according to the power at work within us, to him be glory in the church and in Christ Jesus throughout all generations, forever and ever. Amen" (Eph 3:20–21).

Bibliography

Propositions and Conclusions concerning the True Christian Religion, containing a Confession of faith of certain English people, living at Amsterdam. 1612.

A CONFESSION OF FAITH of seven congregations or churches of Christ in London, which are commonly, but unjustly, called Anabaptists; published for the vindication of the truth and information of the ignorant; likewise for the taking off those aspersions which are frequently, both in pulpit and print, unjustly cast upon them. London, 1644.

A CONFESSION OF FAITH of seven congregations or churches of Christ in London, which are commonly, but unjustly, called Anabaptists; published for the vindication of the truth and information of the ignorant; likewise for the taking off those aspersions which are frequently, both in pulpit and print, unjustly cast upon them. 2nd ed. London, 1646.

The Petition of the Jewes for the Repealing of the Act of Parliament for their banishment out of England. Presented to his Excellency and the generall Councell of Officers on Fryday Jan. 5. 1648. London, 1648.

Declaration of Several of the People Called Anabaptists In and About the City of London... London, 1659.

Declaration of Several Baptized Believers walking in all the foundation principles... London, 1659.

A Declaration of Some of those People in or near London called Anabaptists... London, 1660.

Behold a cry! or, A true relation of the inhumane and violent outrages of divers souldiers, constables, and others, practised upon many of the Lord's people, commonly (though falsly) called Anabaptists, at their several meetings in and about London... London, 1662.

THE BAPTIST CONFESSION OF FAITH With Scripture Proofs Adopted by the Ministers and Messengers of the General Assembly Which Met in London. London, 1689.

Arnold, Samuel Greene. *History of the State of Rhode Island and Providence Plantations: 1636-1700, Vol I.* New York: Appleton and Broadway, 1859.

Baines, Arnold H. J. "Innocency Vindicated; or, Reproach Wip'd Off." *The Baptist Quarterly*, 16, No. 4 (October, 1955): 167.

Baptist Union Publication Department. "Notes and Query." In *Transactions of the Baptist Historical Society*, 3, No. 3 (May, 1913): 190–192.

Bibliography

Bartels, Emily C. "Too Many Blackamoors: Deportation, Discrimination, and Elizabeth I." *Studies in English Literature, 1500-1900*, 46, No. 2 (spring, 2006): 305–322.

Bell, Mark R. *Apocalypse How?: Baptist Movements during the English Revolution*. Macon: Mercer, 2000.

Bickley, Augustus Charles. "Helwys, Thomas". In *Dictionary of National Biography, Vol. 25, Harris—Henry I*. Edited by Leslie Stephen and Sidney Lee, 375–376. New York: Macmillan and Co., 1891.

Bingham, Matthew C. *Orthodox Radicals: Baptist Identity in the English Revolution*. Oxford: Oxford University Press, 2019.

Blackwood, Christopher. *Storming of Antichrist in his two last and strongest Garrisons, of Compulsion of Conscience and Infants Baptisme...* London, 1644.

Blackwood, Christopher. *Apostolicall baptisme: or, A sober rejoinder, to a treatise written by Mr. Thomas Blake; intituled, Infants baptisme freed from Antichristianisme...* London, 1645.

Blackwood, Christopher. *Exposition of Matthew Chapters One to Ten*. London, 1659.

Bradford, William. *Of Plymouth Plantation: 1620-1647*. New York: Modern Library, 1952.

Brady, Gary. *The Great Ejection 1662: Today's Evangelicalism Rooted in Puritan Persecution*. Darlington: Evangelical Press, 2012.

Brotton, Jerry. *This Orient Isle: Elizabethan England and the Islamic World*. London: Allen Lane, 2016.

Brown, Douglas. "Christopher Blackwood: Portrait of a Seventeenth Century Baptist." *Baptist Quarterly*, 32, No. 1 (January, 1987): 28–38.

Browning, Andrew. "Declaration of Indulgence of King James II, April 4, 1687". *English Historical Documents*, 8. London: Eyre and Spottiswoode, 1953.

Burrage, Champlin. "The Fifth Monarchy Insurrections." In *The English Historical Review, Vol. 25*, Issue C, edited by Reginald L. Poole, 722–747. London: Longmans, Greene And Co., 1910.

Busher, Leonard. "Religion's Peace: A Plea for Liberty of Conscience." In *Tracts on Liberty of Conscience and Persecution 1614-1661*. Edited by Edward B. Underhill. 1–83. London: J. Haddon, 1846.

Capp, Bernard. *The Fifth Monarchy Men: A Study in Seventeenth Century Millenarianism*. London: Faber and Faber, 2011.

Carr, Matthew. *Blood and faith: the purging of Muslim Spain, 1492-1614*. London: Hurst & Company, 2017.

Catherwood, Christopher. *Church History: A Crash Course for the Curious*. Wheaton: Crossway Books, 2007.

Charles II, King of England. *His declaration to all his loving subjects of the kingdom of England. Dated from his Court at Breda in Holland, the 4/14 of April 1660. And read in Parliament, May, 1. 1660. Together with his Majesties letter of the same date, to his Excellence the Lord General Monck, to be communicated to the Lord President of the Council of State, and to the officers of the army under his command*. Reprint, by Christopher Higgins, in Harts Close, over against the Trone-Church, Edinburgh, 1660.

Charles II, King of England. *A Proclamation for the Suppression of Coffee-Houses*. London: John Bill and Christopher Barker, 1675.

Christian, John T. *Did they dip? or, An examination into the act of baptism as practiced by the English and American Baptists before the year 1641*. Louisville: Baptist Book Concern, 1896.

Chute, Anthony L., Nathan A. Finn, and Michael A. G. Haykin eds. *The Baptist Story: From English Sect to Global Movement*. Nashville: B&H Publishing, 2015.

Coffey, John. "Puritanism and Liberty Revisited: The Case for Toleration in the English Revolution." *Historical Journal*, 41, No. 4 (December, 1998): 961–985.

Collier, Thomas. *The Exaltation of Christ in the Dayes of the Gospel: as the alone High-Priest, Prophet, and King, of Saints*. London, 1646.

Collins, Hercules. *Counsel for the living, occasioned from the dead, or, A discourse on Job III, 17, 18 arising from the deaths of Mr. Fran. Bampfield and Mr. Zach. Ralphson*. London, 1684.

Cowan, Brian. *The Social Life of Coffee: The Emergence of the British Coffeehouse*. New Haven: Yale, 2005.

Coxe, Nehemia. *Vindiciæ veritatis, or, A confutation - the heresies and gross errours asserted by Thomas Collier in his additional word to his body of divinity*. London, 1677.

Cromwell, Oliver. "Speech III," First Parliament, 12 September 1656. In *Oliver Cromwell's Letters and Speeches, Vol. 2*, edited by Thomas Carlyle, 106–132. New York: Harper and Brothers, 1868.

Cross, Anthony R. "The Adoption of Believer's Baptism and Baptist Beginnings." In *Exploring Baptist Origins*, edited by Anthony R. Cross and Nicholas J. Wood, 1-31. Oxford: Centre for Baptist History and Heritage, Regents Park College, 2010.

Cross, Frank L. "Helwys, Thomas." In *The Oxford Dictionary of the Christian Church*, 3rd. rev. ed, edited by Elizabeth A. Livingstone, 753-754. Oxford: University Press, 2005.

Dasent, John Roche, ed. *Acts of the Privy Council of England*, n.s., Vol. 26, 1596–1597. London: Macklemore, 1902.

DeYoung, Kevin. "The Rise of Right-Wing Wokeism." Review of *The Case for Christian Nationalism*, Stephen Wolfe. *The Gospel Coalition*, November 2022.

Duesing, Jason G., Thomas White, and Malcolm B. Yarnell III, eds. *First Freedom: The Beginning and End of Religious Liberty*, 2nd ed. Nashville, TN: B&H Academic, 2016.

Bibliography

Durso, Keith E. *No Armor for the Back: Baptist Prison Writings, 1600s-1700s.* Macon: Mercer, 2007.

Eberstadt, Mary. *It's Dangerous to Believe: Religious Freedom and Its Enemies.* San Francisco: Harper, 2016.

Edwards, Thomas. *The Second Part of Gangraena: Or a Catalog and Discovery of many of the Errours, Heresies, Blasphemies, and pernicious Practices of the Sectaries of this time.* London, 1646.

Fiddes, Paul S. "Church and Sect: Cross-Currents in Early Baptist Life." In *Exploring Baptist Origins.* Edited by Anthony R. Cross and Nicholas J. Wood. Oxford: Regent's Park College, 2010.

Fraser, Antonia. *The Gunpowder Plot: Terror and Faith in 1605.* London: Weidenfeld and Nicolson, 1996.

Garrett, James L. *Baptist Theology.* Macon: Mercer University Press, 2009.

Gray, Matthew James. "'Baptism, No Wall of Division': Seventeenth-Century Particular Baptists and Dynamics of Toleration." D.Phil. thesis, University of Adelaide, 2018.

Gribben, Crawford. "Baptists and Millennialism in Early Modern England". In *Exploring Baptist Origins.* Edited by Anthony R. Cross and Nicholas J. Wood. Oxford: Centre for Baptist History and Heritage, Regents Park College, 2010.

Goodrich, Luke. *Free to Believe: The Battle Over Religious Liberty in America.* Colorado Springs: Multnomah, 2019.

Haykin, Michael A.G. *Kiffen, Knollys, and Keach: Rediscovering our English Baptist Heritage.* Peterborough: H&E, 2019.

Haykin, Michael A.G. *The British Particular Baptists 1638-1910, Vol. 1.* Springfield: Particular Baptist Press, 1998.

Haykin, Michael A.G. *The Weekly Historian: 52 Reflections on Church History.* Peterborough: H&E, 2021.

Haymes, Brian. "'Thomas Helwys' The Mystery of Iniquity: Is it still relevant in the Twenty-First Century." In *Exploring Baptist Origins*, edited by Anthony R. Cross and Nicholas J. Wood, 61-77. Oxford: Centre for Baptist History and Heritage, Regents Park College, 2010.

Helwys, Thomas. *A Short Declaration of the Mistery of Iniquity.* London, 1611/1612.

Holland, Tom. *Dominion: How the Christian Revolution Remade the World.* New York: Basic Books, 2019.

Hubmaier, Balthasar. "On Heretics and Those who Burn Them". In *Balthasar Hubmaier: Theologian of Anabaptism*, translated and edited by H. Wayne Pipkin and John Howard Yoder, 59-66. Scottdale: Herald, 1989.

Hughes, Paul L. and James F. Larkin eds. "Licensing Casper van Senden to Deport Negroes [draft]. Ca. January 1601." In *Tudor Royal Proclamations, Vol. 3, The Later Tudors (1588-1603)*, 221-222. New Haven and London: Yale University Press, 1969.

Hulse, Erroll. *An Introduction to the Baptists*. Haywards Heath: Carey Publications, 1976.

James, Sharon. *How Christianity Transformed the World*. Fearn: Christian Focus, 2021.

Johnson, Ronald A. "The Peculiar Ventures of Particular Baptist Pastor William Kiffin and King Charles II of England." *Baptist History and Heritage*, 44, No. 1 (winter, 2009): 60-71.

Keach, Benjamin. *Sion in distress: or, The groans of the Protestant Church*. London, 1681.

Kiffin, William, et al. "The Humble Petition And Representation Of Several Churches of God in London, Commonly (though Falsly) Called the Anabaptists. Which was Presented on Monday the Second of April, to the Supream Authority of the Nation, the Commons Assembled in Parliament. Together with the Answer and Appropriation of the Parliament Thereunto." In *Confessions of Faith, and Other Public Documents, Illustrative of the History of the Baptist Churches of England in the 17th Century*, edited by Edward Bean Underhill, 288-311. London: Haddon Brothers, and Co., Castle Street, Finsbury, 1649.

Kiffin, William, et al. *The humble apology of some commonly called Anabaptists, in behalf of themselves and others of the same judgement with them: with their protestation against the late wicked and most horrid treasonable insurrection and rebellion acted in the city of London. Together with an apology formerly presented to the Kings most Excellent Majesty*. London: Henry Hills, 1661.

Knolles, Richard. *The Generall Historie of the Turkes, from the first beginning of that nation to the rising of the Othoman Familie: with all the notable expeditions of the Christian princes against them, together with the liues and conquests of the othoman kings and emperours faithfullie collected out of the best histories, both auntient and moderne, and digested into one continuat historie untill this present yeare 1603*. London: Adam Islip, 1603.

Kreitzer, Larry. *William Kiffen and his World (Part 4)*, Re-sourcing Baptist History: Seventeenth Century Series, Vols. 1-6. Regent's Park College: Oxford, 2010-2017.

LaFantasie, Glenn W. ed. "The Road to Banishment: Editorial Note." In *The Correspondence of Roger Williams, Vol. 1, 1629-1653*, 12-23. Hanover: Brown University Press, 1988.

LaFantasie, Glenn W. ed. *The Correspondence of Roger Williams, Vol. 2, 1654-1683*. Hanover: Brown University Press, 1988.

Land, Richard Dale. "Doctrinal Controversies of English Particular Baptists (1644-1691) as Illustrated by the Career and Writings of Thomas Collier." D.Phil. diss., University of Oxford, 1979.

Lumpkin, William L. *Baptist Confessions of Faith, Second Revised Edition*. Edited by Bill J. Leonard. Valley Forge: Judson Press, 2011.

Bibliography

Macauley, Thomas Babbington. *The History of England from the Accession of James II,* Vols. 1-2. London: Folio Society, 2009.

MacLean, Gerald M. and Nabil Matar. *Britain and the Islamic World, 1558-1713.* Oxford: Oxford University Press, 2011.

Marlow, Isaac. "James Jones's Coffee-House." *Baptist Quarterly*, 6, No. 7 (July, 1933): 324-326.

Matzko, Paul. "Beware the 'Christian Prince.'" Review of *The Case for Christian Nationalism*, Stephen Wolfe. *Reason*, June 2023.

McBeth, Leon. *English Baptist Literature on Religious Liberty to 1689.* New York: Arno, 1980.

Melo, João Vicente. "Roderigo Lopez (c.1525-1594)." In *Lives in Transit in Early Modern England: Identity and Belonging.* Edited by Nandini Das. Amsterdam: University Press, 2022.

Milton, John. *On the New Forcers of Conscience under the Long Parliament.* London, 1646.

Monck, Thomas, et al. *An Orthodox creed, or, A Protestant confession of faith: being an essay to unite and confirm all true Protestants in the fundamental articles of the Christian religion, against the errors and heresies of the church of Rome.* London, 1679.

Needham, Nicholas R. *2000 Years of Christ's Power, Part Three: Renaissance and Reformation.* London: Grace Publications Trust, 2004.

Needham, Nicholas R. *2000 Years of Christ's Power, Part Four: The Age of Religious Conflict.* London: Grace Publications Trust, 2016.

Nelson, Stanley E. "Reflecting on Baptist Origins: The London Confession of Faith of 1644." *Baptist History and Heritage*, 29, No. 2 (April, 1994): 33-46.

Panter, Paul L. "Reclaiming Christopher Blackwood for Baptist Historiography: A Pioneer for Particular Baptists and the Oracle of the English Baptists to Ireland 1605-1670." D.Phil. diss., Midwestern Baptist Theological Seminary, 2022.

Paul II, John. Letter to the heads of state of the nations who signed the Helsinki Final Act (1975). On the eve of the Madrid Conference on European Security and Cooperation, September 1, 1980.

Petrik, Jennifer. '"Falsely Called Anabaptists": The Particular Baptist Doctrine of Baptism.' Diss, Westminster Seminary California, December 2009.

Raithby, John. ed. *Statutes of the Realm: Vol. 5, 1628-80.* N.p., 1819.

Ramsbottom, B. A. *Stranger than Fiction: the Life of William Kiffin.* Harpenden: Gospel Standard Trust Publications, 1989.

Randall, Ian M. "Early English Baptists and Religious Liberty." *Anabaptism Today*, No. 4 (October, 1993).

Randall, Ian M. *Communities of Conviction: Baptist Beginnings in Europe.* Schwarzenfeld: Neufeld Verlag, 2009.

Randall, Ian M. "Baptists, The Gospel and Freedom of Conscience." In *50th Anniversary Lecture of the SBHS*. Dunstable: Fauconberg Press, 2010.

Renihan, James M. "Thomas Collier's Descent Into Error: Collier, Calvinism, and the Second London Confession." *Reformed Baptist Theological Review*, 1, No. 1 (January, 2004): 67–84.

Renihan, James M. "Confessing the Faith in 1644 and 1689." *Reformed Baptist Theological Review*, 3, No. 1 (January, 2006): 27–47.

Renihan, James M. "The Strange Case of Thomas Collier." *Journal of the Institute of Reformed Baptist Studies*, 3, No. 1 (November, 2016): 97–122.

Richardson, Samuel. *The necessity of toleration in matters of religion, or, Certain questions propounded to the Synod, tending to prove that corporall punishments ought not to be inflicted upon such as hold errors in religion, and that in matters of religion, men ought not to be compelled, but have liberty and freedome.: Here is also the copy of the edict of the Emperours Constantinus and Licinius, and containing the reasons that inforced them to grant unto all men liberty to choose, and follow what religion they thought best. Also here is the faith of the Assembly of Divines, as it was taken out of the exactest copy of their practise, with the nonconformists answer why they cannot receive and submit to the said faith*. London, 1647.

Roberts, Mostyn. *The Subversive Puritan: Roger Williams and Freedom of Conscience*. Darlington: Evangelical Press, 2019.

Robinson, H. Wheeler. "The Five Points of a Baptist's Faith". *The Baptist Quarterly*, n.s., 11, Nos. 1-2 (1942-1945): 4–14.

Scott, James, duke of Monmouth. *The declaration of James Duke of Monmouth, & the noblemen, gentlemen & others, now in arms, for defence & vindication of the Protestant religion, & the laws, rights, & privilieges of England, from the invasion made upon them, & for delivering the kingdom from the usurpation & tyranny of James Duke of York*. London, 1685.

Siedentop, Larry. *Inventing the Individual: The Origins of Western Liberalism*. New York: Allen Lane, 2014.

Sowerby, Scott. *Making Toleration: The Repealers and the Glorious Revolution*. Cambridge, MA: Harvard University Press, 2013.

Spilsbury, John. His personal confession of ten articles for the *"Godly reader to judge, what difference there is between him and me, in the main, that men should be so incensed against me, as to seek my life, as some have done."* London, 1643.

Spurgeon, C. H. "A Blast of the Trumpet against False Peace." In *The New Park Street Pulpit Sermons, Vol. 6*. London: Passmore and Alabaster, 1860.

Spurgeon, C. H. *The Sword and Trowel: 1873*. London: Passmore & Alabaster, 1873.

Staples, William R. *Annals of the Town of Providence, from Its First Settlement, to the Organization of the City Government*, 30–31. Providence: Knowles and Vose, 1843.

Bibliography

Stoddard, Jennifer R. "Seventeenth Century Particular Baptist Views on Religious Liberty." MA thesis, Westminster Seminary California, 2011.

Tait, William and Christian Isobel Johnstone eds. "The Life and Rebellion of the Duke of Monmouth." *Tait's Edinburgh Magazine*, January 1845, 50-60.

Taylor, A. *The English General Baptists of the Seventeenth Century*. London, 1815.

Thomas, Henry. *The Ancient Remains, Antiquities, and Recent Improvements, of the City of London: Containing a Full Description of the Several Wards, Parishes, Precincts, Churches, Halls, and Other Public Buildings, and Curiosities, Ancient and Modern-- to which is Added, a List of Aldermen and Mayors Since the Revolution, Vol. 2*. London: Sears, 1830.

Tolan, John V. "The first imposition of a badge on European Jews: the English royal mandate of 1218." In *The Character of Christian-Muslim Encounter: Essays in honour of David Thomas*. Edited by Douglas Pratt, Jon Hoover, John Davies, and John A. Chesworth. Netherlands: Brill, 2016.

Tolan, John V. *Faces of Muhammad: Western Perceptions of the Prophet of Islam from the Middle Ages to Today*. Princeton: Princeton University Press, 2019.

Traffanstedt, Chris. "A Primer on Baptist History: The True Baptist Trail." *The Reformed Reader*. November 16, 2022. http://www.reformedreader.org/history/pbh.htm.

Waldron, Samuel E. *A Modern Exposition of the 1689 Baptist Confession of Faith*, 3rd ed. Reprint, with a new preface, Darlington: Evangelical Press, 2005.

Walker, Andrew T. *Liberty for All: Defending Everyone's Religious Freedom in a Pluralistic Age*. Grand Rapids: Brazos Press, 2021.

Walker, Andrew T. "Book Review: The Case for Christian Nationalism." Review of *The Case for Christian Nationalism*, Stephen Wolfe. *Nine Marks*, November 2022.

Warren, James A. *God, War, and Providence: the epic struggle of Roger Williams and the Narragansett Indians against the Puritans of New England*. New York: Scribner, 2018.

Weidl, Birgit. "Anti-Jewish legislation in the Middle Ages." In *Comprehending Antisemitism through the Ages: A Historical Perspective*. Edited by Armin Lange, Kerstin Mayerhofer, Dina Porat, and Lawrence H. Schiffman. Boston: DeGruyter, 2021.

Weissbourd, Emily. "'Those in Their Possession': Race, Slavery, and Queen Elizabeth's "Edicts of Expulsion."' *Huntington Library Quarterly*, 78, No. 1 (spring, 2015): 1-19.

White, Barrie R. "Early Baptist Arguments for Religious Freedom: Their Overlooked Agenda." *Baptist History and Heritage*, 24, No. 4 (October, 1989): 3-10.

White, Barrie R. *The English Baptists of the Seventeenth Century, A History of the English Baptists 1*, 2nd rev. ed. Didcot, Oxfordshire: The Baptist Historical Society, 1996.

White, Thomas. "'The Defense of Religious Liberty' by the Anabaptists and the English Baptists." In *First Freedom: The Baptist Perspective on Religious Liberty*. Edited by Thomas White, Jason B. Duesing, and Malcolm B. Yarnell III. Nashville: B&H, 2007.

Whitley, William Thomas. *A Baptist Bibliography, Vol. I*. Hildesheim: Georg Olms, 1984.

Wilken, Robert Louis. *Liberty in the Things of God: The Christian Origins of Religious Freedom*. New Haven: Yale University Press, 2019.

Williams, Roger. "To the truly Christian reader." In *The fourth paper, presented by Major Butler, to the Honourable Committee of Parliament, for the propagating the gospel of Christ Jesus* (1651).

Williams, Roger. *The Bloudy Tenent of Persecution for Cause of Conscience*. Edited by S. L. Caldwell. R.I.: Providence, The Narragansett Club, 1867.

Williams, Roger. "A Biographical Introduction." In *The Bloudy Tenent of Persecution for Cause of Conscience Discussed and Mr. Cotton's Letter Examined and Answered*. Edited by Edward Bean Underhill, v–xxxvi. Kessinger Publishing, 2004.

Williams, Roger. "Christenings make not Christians." In *On Religious Liberty: Selections from the Works of Roger Williams*. Edited by James Calvin Davis. Harvard: University Press, 2008.

Williamson, G. I. *The Westminster Confession of Faith for Study Classes*, 2nd ed. Phillipsburg: P&R Publishing, 2004.

Winthrop, John. *Winthrop's Journal: 1630-1649 volume I*. Edited by James K. Hosmer. New York: Charles Scribner's Sons, 1908.

Witte, Jr., John and Frank S. Alexander, eds. *Christianity and Human Rights: An Introduction*. Cambridge: Cambridge University Press, 2010.

Wolfe, Stephen. *The Case for Christian Nationalism*. Moscow: Canon Press, 2022.

Wright, Stephen. *The Early English Baptists, 1603-1649*. New York: Boydell Press, 2006.

Yarbrough, Slayden A. "The English Separatist Influence on the Baptist Tradition of Church-State Issues." *Baptist History and Heritage*, 20, No. 3 (July, 1985): 14–23.

Yarnell III, Malcolm B. "The Development of Religious Liberty: A Survey of its Progress and Challenges in Christian History." *Journal for Baptist Theology and Ministry*, 6, No. 1 (spring, 2009): 119–138.

Yarnell III, Malcolm B. "'We Believe with the Heart and with the Mouth Confess': The Engaged Piety of the Early General Baptists" in *The Baptist Quarterly* 44(1), 36-58 (2011)

Bibliography

Yarnell III, Malcolm B. "Political Theology among the Earliest Baptists: The Foundational Contribution of Leonard Busher, 1614-1646," in John H. Y. Briggs and Anthony R. Cross, *Freedom and the Powers: Perspectives from Baptist History Marking the 400th Anniversary of Thomas Helwys' The Mystery of Iniquity* (London: Baptist Historical Society, 2014)

Yarnell III, Malcolm B. "Christopher Blackwood: Exemplar of the Seventeenth-Century Particular Baptists." *Southwestern Journal of Theology*, 57, No. 2 (spring, 2015): 181–205.

York, Tripp. *The Purple Crown: the Politics of* Martyrdom. Scottdale, PA: Herald Press, 2007.

He put another parable before them, saying,

"The kingdom of heaven may be compared to a man who sowed good seed in his field, but while his men were sleeping, his enemy came and sowed weeds among the wheat and went away. So when the plants came up and bore grain, then the weeds appeared also. And the servants of the master of the house came and said to him, 'Master, did you not sow good seed in your field? How then does it have weeds?' He said to them, 'An enemy has done this.' So the servants said to him, 'Then do you want us to go and gather them?' But he said, 'No, lest in gathering the weeds you root up the wheat along with them. Let both grow together until the harvest, and at harvest time I will tell the reapers, "Gather the weeds first and bind them in bundles to be burned, but gather the wheat into my barn."'"

… Then he left the crowds and went into the house.
And his disciples came to him, saying,

"Explain to us the parable of the weeds of the field." He answered, "The one who sows the good seed is the Son of Man. The field is the world, and the good seed is the sons of the kingdom. The weeds are the sons of the evil one, and the enemy who sowed them is the devil. The harvest is the end of the age, and the reapers are angels. Just as the weeds are gathered and burned with fire, so will it be at the end of the age. The Son of Man will send his angels, and they will gather out of his kingdom all causes of sin and all law-breakers, and throw them into the fiery furnace. In that place there will be weeping and gnashing of teeth. Then the righteous will shine like the sun in the kingdom of their Father.
He who has ears, let him hear."

Matthew 13:24–30, 36–43

Subject Index

1644 *Confession*. *See First London Baptist Confession*
Act of Toleration, 15, 95, 99
Act of Uniformity, 68, 85
American Baptists, vii, 107
Anabaptist, 8, 9, 10, 14, 25, 28, 33, 39, 47, 50, 60, 70, 71, 105, 108, 109, 110, 113
Anglicanism, 3, 13, 53, 63, 71, 73, 93
Arminianism, 99
Augustine, vii, 27
Bampfield, Francis, 91
Baptism, vi, 1, 2, 9, 10, 25, 28, 49, 55, 59, 70, 73, 80, 97, 98, 100, 107
Battle of Sedgemoor, 92
Blackwood, Christopher, 50, 71, 73, 75, 98, 106, 110, 114
Blaurock, George, 9, 10
Bloody Assizes, 92
Book of Common Prayer, 32, 68
Busher, Leonard, 23, 37, 38, 39, 40, 41, 42, 45, 46, 106, 114
Calvin, John, vii, 3, 10, 27, 28, 75, 113
Charles I, 61, 67
Charles II, 14, 67, 69, 70, 79, 85, 91, 92, 93, 106, 107, 109
Christendom, 1, 11, 54

Christian Nationalism, iv, 4, 19, 97, 107, 110, 112, 113
Church and state, 1, vi, 9, 25, 32, 80
Church membership, 9, 28
Church of England, 12, 26, 39, 40, 53, 68, 94, 95, 98
Clarendon Code, 68
Coffee houses, 69, 94
Collier, Thomas, 79, 80, 81, 82, 86, 94, 107, 109, 111
Collins, Hercules, 91
Colonisation, 55
Continental Anabaptists, vii
Conventicle Act, 68, 85
Cornwell, Francis, 73
Corporation Act, 68, 85
Coxe, Nehemiah, 82, 93, 94, 107
Cranmer, Thomas, 26
Cromwell, Oliver, 13, 65, 66, 67, 70, 85, 107
Dominionism, 4
Ecclesiology, 9
Edward I, 16, 19, 20
Edwards, Thomas, 59, 80
Elizabeth I, 18, 19, 106
English Separatism, 25
English Separatists, 10
Erastianism, 80
Evangelism, 1, 2, 10, 79

Fifth Monarchy, 50, 64, 67, 70, 106
First London Baptist Confession, 59, 79, 80, 81, 82
Five Mile Act, 68
Five-Mile Act, 85
General Baptists, 5, 17, 23, 33, 45, 46, 49, 50, 53, 65, 70, 71, 73, 74, 77, 87, 98, 99, 105, 107, 112, 113
Great Persecution, 91
Grebel, Conrad, 9, 10
Helwys, Joan, 13
Helwys, Thomas, viii, 1, 6, 10, 13, 25, 30, 31, 32, 33, 34, 37, 42, 45, 49, 56, 106, 107, 108, 114
Hewling, Benjamin, 79
Hewling, William, 79
Holy Spirit, v, vii, 2, 10, 37, 38, 57, 89
Hubmaier, Balthasar, 9, 10, 33, 39, 108
Hubmaier, Elisabeth, 10
Indians. *See* Indigenous tribes
Indigenous tribes, 54, 101
Islam, 17, 19, 66, 75, 112
Jacob, Henry, 49
James I, 30, 32, 36, 41, 54
James II, 90, 91, 92, 93, 94, 95, 106, 110
Jessey, Henry, 49
JLJ Church, 49
Jones, James, 69, 94, 110
Judaism, 1, 4, 15, 16, 17, 19, 20, 32, 40, 41, 42, 56, 66, 67, 74, 77, 80, 112
Keach, Benjamin, 12, 85
Ketch, Jack, 92
Kiffen, William, 50, 70, 78, 79, 80, 82, 91, 92, 93, 95, 108, 109
Knolles, Richard, 17
Knollys, Hanserd, 79, 80
Knox, John, 3
Lambe, Thomas, 70
Legate, Bartholomew, 13
Lopez, Rodrigo, 20
Lord's Supper, vi
Lothrop, John, 49
Luther, Martin, 3, 10, 27
Lutheranism, 28
Mantz, Felix, 9, 10
Marsden, Jeremiah, 91
Massachusetts Bay Company, 54
Media, 3, 97
Mennonites, 25, 31
Milton, John, 63
Monmouth Rebellion, 79
Murton, John, 45, 46, 49, 53, 56
Muslims, 4, 18, 19, 40, 74, 75
Narragansett tribe, 55
Natives. *See* Indigenous tribes
Ottoman Empire, 17, 18, 66
Paedobaptism, 1, 98
Particular Baptists, 5, 46, 47, 49, 53, 65, 71, 73, 74, 80, 86, 87, 94, 99, 108, 109, 110, 114
Penn, William, vii, 94
Persecution, 1, v, vii, 3, 4, 10, 13, 15, 19, 21, 26, 27, 31, 32, 37, 39, 50, 55, 56, 62, 65, 70, 73, 74, 75, 79, 99
Politics, 71, 93
Pope John Paul II, iii

Presbyterianism, 1, 3, 57, 59, 63, 71, 80, 85, 86, 97
Puritans, iv, vii, 3, 25, 26, 53, 54, 106, 111, 112
Quakers, vii
Quran, 66
Racism, v, 18
Ralphson, Zachariah. *See* Marsden, Jeremiah
Reconstructionism, 4
Reformers, vi, 26, 27
Regeneration, 9, 37, 39, 63, 89
Religious liberty, 1, 2, iv, 2, 5, 6, 14, 17, 21, 26, 27, 28, 32, 33, 34, 37, 40, 41, 42, 46, 50, 53, 54, 55, 59, 61, 63, 65, 66, 67, 71, 77, 80, 82, 85, 86, 96, 98, 99, 100, 101
Revolution, 70, 71
Richardson, Samuel, 61, 62, 63
Ridley, Nicholas, 26
Roman Catholicism, iii, 9, 10, 11, 14, 15, 18, 19, 27, 33, 39, 40, 41, 45, 71, 75, 76, 77, 79, 93, 95, 97
Sattler, Michael, 10
Scott, James, 92
Second London Baptist Confession, 79, 85, 99
Second London Baptist Confession of Faith, 95
Separatism, 25, 50
Slavery, 17
Smyth, John, 13, 24, 25, 26, 27, 28, 31, 33, 37, 42, 45
Spanish Inquisition, 20
Spilsbury, John, 48, 61, 79, 91
Spurgeon, C.H, 4
Spurgeon, C.H., 99
Standard Confession, 5
State-church, 1, 13, 53, 54, 55
Sufficiency of Scripture, v
Süleyman the Magnificent, 17
Sultan Murad III, 18
Test Act, 85
Theonomy, 4
United States, 3, 104
Venner, Thomas, 64, 70
Walter, Lucy, 92
Westminster Confession, 86, 113
Whitehall Conference, 67
William III, 95
William of Orange, 95
Williams, Roger, 52, 53, 54, 55, 57, 59, 66, 100, 101, 109, 111, 112, 113
Winthrop, John, 53, 55
Xenophobia, 19
Zwingli, Ulrich, 3, 9, 10, 27, 28

www.ingramcontent.com/pod-product-compliance
Lightning Source LLC
Chambersburg PA
CBHW030554080526
44585CB00012B/378